A Christian Counseling Handbook

Written By

Raymond Joseph Pierlioni

Contents

Chapter 1: Introduction

1.1 Definition of Christian Counseling

Christian counseling is a therapeutic approach that seeks to incorporate Christian principles and beliefs into the counseling process. This approach provides a more comprehensive and multidimensional approach to therapy that addresses not just the physical, emotional, and spiritual needs of individuals, but also their social and cultural needs. Christian counselors believe that God is the ultimate source of healing and that a person's relationship with God is a crucial component of their mental and emotional well-being. They encourage individuals to delve deeper into their personal beliefs and values and to integrate their faith into every aspect of their lives, including their relationships, work, and leisure activities.

One of the primary techniques of Christian counseling is to help individuals develop healthier and more meaningful relationships. Counselors work with clients to teach them how to communicate more effectively and resolve conflicts in a healthy and constructive way. They also help clients explore their identity and self-worth, and how these relate to their relationships with others. By fostering a deeper understanding of themselves and their values, individuals can build stronger and more fulfilling relationships.

For clients who are experiencing symptoms of depression or anxiety, cognitive-behavioral therapy is an effective method. This approach helps individuals identify and modify negative thinking patterns and behaviors that contribute to their symptoms. It also empowers individuals to take control of their thoughts and feelings, and to develop coping strategies for managing stress and anxiety. Support group involvement and counseling can also be beneficial for individuals struggling with addiction. This provides a supportive and non-judgmental environment where individuals can openly discuss their struggles and gain encouragement to overcome them. Christian counselors can also help individuals cope with grief and loss by helping them work through their emotions and find comfort in their faith. This includes exploring how their beliefs about death and the afterlife can provide comfort and hope during difficult times.

In addition to these techniques, Christian counselors can incorporate prayer and scripture into the counseling process. This can provide clients with a deeper understanding of themselves and their relationship with God, which can facilitate long-lasting growth and healing. Christian counseling emphasizes the importance of integrating faith into all aspects of life, and encourages individuals to cultivate a more profound relationship with God. It is a process that aims to help individuals discover their true purpose and meaning in life, to become their best selves, and to live the life they were meant to live. By embracing Christian principles and values, individuals can find greater peace, happiness, and fulfillment in their lives. Christian counseling is not only a therapeutic approach, but also a way of life that can transform individuals and communities.

1.2 Importance of Christian Counseling in Today's World

Christian counseling plays a crucial role in addressing mental health issues in today's world. According to the

National Institute of Mental Health, one in five adults in the United States experiences mental illness each year. Christian counseling provides an alternative approach to traditional therapy by incorporating faith and spirituality into the counseling process. This approach can be especially beneficial for individuals who find comfort and healing in their relationship with God.

Christian counseling also addresses the unique needs of individuals who identify as Christians. For example, individuals may struggle with feelings of guilt or shame related to their faith. Christian counselors can help individuals work through these emotions and find healing and forgiveness through their relationship with God.

Another benefit of Christian counseling is the emphasis on community and support. Christian counselors can provide individuals with a safe and supportive environment to discuss their struggles and receive encouragement to overcome them. This support can be especially important for individuals who may feel isolated or alone in their struggles.

Overall, Christian counseling provides a holistic approach to mental health that addresses not only the physical and emotional needs but also the spiritual needs of individuals. It can be a powerful tool for individuals seeking healing and growth in their lives.

1.3 Overview of the Manual

This manual provides a comprehensive guide to Christian counseling, including theological foundations, counseling techniques, and ethical considerations. It is intended for individuals who are interested in pursuing a career in

Christian counseling, as well as for current counselors who wish to deepen their understanding of the integration of faith and psychology.

The manual is organized into fifteen chapters, each of which covers a different aspect of Christian counseling. Chapter 1 provides an introduction to Christian counseling, including its definition and importance in today's world. Chapter 2 explores the theological foundations of Christian counseling, including the biblical basis and the role of the Holy Spirit. Chapter 3 discusses the counseling process, including understanding the client, the role of the counselor, and ethical considerations.

Chapters 4 through 6 cover specific issues, techniques, and approaches in Christian counseling, including marriage and family counseling, addiction counseling, and cognitive-behavioral therapy. Chapter 7 focuses on Christian counseling in the church, including the role of the church and lay counseling programs. Chapter 8 explores the integration of faith and psychology, including challenges and best practices. Chapters 9 and 10 cover ethical and legal issues in Christian counseling, including the code of ethics and informed consent.

Chapter 11 discusses self-care for Christian counselors, including burnout and compassion fatigue. Chapter 12 covers assessment and testing in Christian counseling, including psychological testing and cultural competence. Chapter 13 examines common mental health disorders in Christian counseling, including medication and referring clients for mental health treatment. Chapter 14 discusses intersectionality in Christian counseling, including race and ethnicity, socioeconomic status, and gender.

Finally, Chapter 15 provides a summary of the manual and future directions for Christian counseling. The manual is designed to be a comprehensive resource for individuals interested in Christian counseling and a guide for current counselors seeking to deepen their practice.

Chapter 2: Theological Foundations of Christian Counseling

2.1 Biblical Basis for Christian Counseling

Christian counseling is a multifaceted approach that integrates biblical principles and psychological theories and methods in a way that aims to provide holistic care to individuals. It recognizes the value and dignity of human beings, the need for healing and restoration, and the role of the Holy Spirit as the counselor and guide.

The practice of Christian counseling is based on a rich foundation of biblical passages that offer a framework for understanding the nature of human beings, their problems, and their potential. The following are some of the biblical references on the subject of counseling:

- Proverbs 11:14 - "Where there is no guidance, a people falls, but in an abundance of counselors there is safety."
- Proverbs 15:22 - "Without counsel plans fail, but with many advisers they succeed."

- Isaiah 9:6 - "For to us a child is born, to us a son is given; and the government shall be upon his shoulder, and his name shall be called Wonderful Counselor, Mighty God, Everlasting Father, Prince of Peace."
- Matthew 7:7-8 - "Ask, and it will be given to you; seek, and you will find; knock, and it will be opened to you. For everyone who asks receives, and the one who seeks finds, and to the one who knocks it will be opened."
- John 14:26 - "But the Helper, the Holy Spirit, whom the Father will send in my name, he will teach you all things and bring to your remembrance all that I have said to you."
- Romans 12:2 - "Do not be conformed to this world, but be transformed by the renewal of your mind, that by testing you may discern what is the will of God, what is good and acceptable and perfect."
- Galatians 6:2 - "Bear one another's burdens, and so fulfill the law of Christ."
- James 1:5 - "If any of you lacks wisdom, let him ask God, who gives generously to all without reproach, and it will be given him."

While Genesis 1:26-27 affirms the value and dignity of human beings, Psalm 139:13-16 provides a sense of comfort and assurance that every individual is loved and cared for by God, and that their life has meaning and purpose. Isaiah 61:1-3 describes the mission of the Messiah, who is Jesus Christ, and calls God's people to participate in this mission by being his agents of healing and restoration in a broken world. John 14:15-17 introduces the Holy Spirit as another counselor who will guide and teach believers after Jesus' departure, providing a basis for the belief that Christian counselors are guided by the Holy Spirit in their work. Finally, 2 Timothy 3:16-17 declares that all Scripture is inspired by God and is useful for teaching, rebuking, correcting, and training in righteousness, providing a foundation for the belief that Scripture is a valuable source of wisdom and guidance in the practice of Christian counseling.

It is important to note that Christian counseling is not limited to these passages and principles. Rather, it is a dynamic and evolving field that seeks to integrate the latest research and techniques in psychology and counseling with the timeless truths of Scripture. Christian counselors are trained to provide a wide range of services, including individual and group therapy, marriage and family counseling, addiction and recovery counseling, and pastoral counseling. They work with individuals of all ages and backgrounds, from children and adolescents to adults and seniors, and they strive to provide compassionate, non-judgmental care that respects the unique needs and circumstances of each person.

In summary, Christian counseling is a holistic approach to care that integrates biblical principles and psychological theories and methods. It is based on a rich foundation of biblical passages that offer a framework for understanding the nature of human beings, their problems, and their potential. Christian counselors are guided by the Holy Spirit and use Scripture as a valuable source of wisdom and guidance in their work. They provide a wide range of services to individuals of all ages and backgrounds, and they strive to provide compassionate, non-judgmental care that respects the unique needs and circumstances of each person.

2.2 The Role of the Holy Spirit in Christian Counseling

One of the essential aspects of Christian counseling is the role of the Holy Spirit. The Holy Spirit is the third person of the Trinity, who is co-equal and co-eternal with the Father and the Son. The Holy Spirit is God's presence and power in the world and in the lives of believers. The Holy Spirit convicts, comforts, teaches, guides, empowers, and transforms those who trust in Christ.

The role of the Holy Spirit in Christian counseling can be understood in different ways. Some of these ways include:

- The Holy Spirit is the counselor's source of wisdom and discernment (1 Corinthians 2:10-16). The counselor needs to rely on the Holy Spirit to understand the counselee's situation, needs, and goals, and to provide biblical and practical solutions. The counselor also needs to be sensitive to the Holy Spirit's leading and prompting in each counseling session, and to follow His direction.
- The Holy Spirit is the counselor's helper and advocate (John 14:26; Romans 8:26-27). The counselor cannot rely on his or her own strength, skills, or knowledge to help the counselee. The counselor needs to depend on the Holy Spirit's help and support in every aspect of the counseling process. The counselor also needs to pray for the Holy Spirit's intervention and assistance for the counselee, and to encourage the counselee to seek the Holy Spirit's guidance and empowerment.
- The Holy Spirit is the counselee's teacher and guide (John 16:13; 1 John 2:27). The counselee needs to learn from the Holy Spirit's instruction and illumination through the Scriptures, which are God's inspired and authoritative Word. The counselee also needs to follow the Holy Spirit's guidance and direction in applying biblical principles and

commands to his or her life. The counselee needs to be open and responsive to the Holy Spirit's voice and work in his or her heart and mind.

- The Holy Spirit is the counselee's healer and transformer (Ezekiel 36:26-27; Galatians 5:22-23). The counselee needs to experience the Holy Spirit's healing and restoration of his or her brokenness, wounds, and hurts. The counselee also needs to undergo the Holy Spirit's transformation of his or her character, attitudes, behaviors, and relationships. The counselee needs to cooperate with the Holy Spirit's sanctifying work in his or her life, which is a lifelong process of becoming more like Christ.

The role of the Holy Spirit in Christian counseling is vital and indispensable. Without the Holy Spirit's involvement, Christian counseling would be ineffective and powerless. With the Holy Spirit's involvement, Christian counseling can be fruitful and impactful. Christian counselors need to be aware of the Holy Spirit's presence and work in their counseling practice and to rely on Him for wisdom, guidance, and empowerment. Biblical references that support the role of the Holy Spirit in Christian counseling include 1 Corinthians 2:10-16, John 14:26, Romans 8:26-27, John 16:13, 1 John 2:27, Ezekiel 36:26-27, and Galatians 5:22-23.

2.3 Integration of Faith and Science in Christian Counseling

Christian counselors face a unique challenge in their work: how to integrate faith and science in a way that is both effective and respectful of the beliefs and values of their clients. Faith and science have often been seen as incompatible or even contradictory, especially in modern secular culture. Some people view faith as irrational, subjective, or based on blind trust, while science is seen as rational, objective, and based on empirical evidence. Others believe that faith and science have different goals or domains, and that they should not interfere with each other. However, Christian counselors have a different perspective on faith and science, seeing them as complementary and harmonious, rather than conflicting or separate.

Christian counselors believe that faith and science are both gifts from God, and that they can work together to reveal His truth and glory. They also believe that faith and science have a common goal: to help people flourish and fulfill their God-given potential. Christian counselors integrate faith and science in various ways in their practice, recognizing that they are not mutually exclusive, but rather two different ways of understanding the world.

- Firstly, Christian counselors use scientific methods and findings to inform their assessment, diagnosis, treatment planning, and evaluation of clients. They keep up with the latest research and developments in their field and apply them to their work. By doing so, they ensure that they are providing the best possible care for their clients. They understand that science provides valuable insight into the human experience, and that it can help them understand the biological, psychological, and social factors that contribute to mental health issues.
- Secondly, Christian counselors use biblical principles and values to guide their ethical decision-making, professional conduct, and relationship with clients. They respect the dignity, worth, and uniqueness of each client as an image-bearer of God. Christian counselors also understand that God

created humans with complex and unique needs. Therefore, they employ a holistic approach to counseling that encompasses the physical, emotional, mental, and spiritual dimensions of the human experience. They believe that Scripture provides valuable guidance and wisdom for how to live a healthy and fulfilling life, and they incorporate these principles into their counseling practice.

- Thirdly, Christian counselors use spiritual interventions and resources to enhance their counseling process and outcomes. They may pray with or for their clients, share relevant scriptures or testimonies, encourage spiritual disciplines or practices, or refer clients to other sources of spiritual support. By incorporating spiritual interventions, Christian counselors provide a unique perspective and approach to counseling that is not found in traditional counseling. They understand that spirituality is an essential aspect of human life, and that it can provide comfort, hope, and meaning during difficult times.
- Lastly, Christian counselors acknowledge the limitations of both faith and science and seek to balance them in their work. They do not rely on either faith or science alone but use them in an integrated way. They recognize that there may be areas of mystery or uncertainty that only God can fully understand, but they continue to seek knowledge and wisdom through both faith and science. They understand that there are some questions that science cannot answer, and that there are some aspects of faith that cannot be explained by science.

In conclusion, Christian counseling is a unique form of professional help that integrates faith and science in a holistic way. Christian counselors seek to honor God with their work and serve their clients with compassion, competence, and integrity. By integrating faith and science, they provide an approach to counseling that is grounded in both biblical truth and scientific evidence, resulting in a comprehensive and effective form of care. Christian counselors understand that faith and science are not mutually exclusive, but rather two different ways of understanding the world, and they seek to use both in a way that is respectful, ethical, and effective.

Chapter 3: The Counseling Process

3.1 Understanding the Client

One of the most important aspects of the counseling process is understanding the client, which is a multifaceted and ongoing process. In order to best serve the client, a strong therapeutic alliance must be established by developing a collaborative and trusting relationship that is built on empathic listening, unconditional positive regard, and a non-judgmental approach. This involves a deep understanding of the client's history and background, including their cultural, social, and economic context, and the ways in which these factors have shaped their beliefs, values, and behaviors. Moreover, it is essential to identify the client's goals and needs, which requires careful assessment of their strengths, challenges, and aspirations. This process involves using a range of counseling techniques and tools, such as standardized assessments, clinical interviews, and self-report measures, to gather comprehensive information about the client's emotional, cognitive, and behavioral functioning. By taking a holistic and client-centered approach, counselors can create a safe and supportive environment that empowers clients to explore their thoughts and feelings, gain insight into their problems, and develop new skills and strategies for personal growth and change.

Building a Relationship

The first step in understanding the client is to build a strong therapeutic relationship. This relationship can be created by the counselor by engaging with the client in a friendly, supportive and welcoming manner. The counselor should aim to make the client feel at ease, and create a safe and secure environment for the client to express their thoughts and feelings. It is important for the counselor to listen carefully to the client and offer empathy, understanding and support. By maintaining a non-judgmental attitude, the counselor can help the client feel comfortable and accepted.

In addition to building a strong therapeutic relationship, the counselor should also be sensitive to the client's cultural and social background. Factors such as ethnicity, religion, gender and sexual orientation can all have an impact on the client's experiences and perspectives. By being aware of these factors, the counselor can better understand the client's thoughts and feelings, and offer guidance and support that is tailored to their unique needs.

To establish a successful counseling relationship, the counselor should also work with the client to establish clear boundaries and expectations. This involves discussing the purpose and goals of counseling, as well as the frequency and duration of sessions. The counselor should also be clear about the limits of confidentiality, and ensure that the client understands their rights and responsibilities in the counseling process. By empowering the client to participate in their own care, the counselor can help them to achieve their goals and make progress towards a more fulfilling life.

In order to gain a more comprehensive understanding of the client, it is important for the counselor to delve into the client's history and background. This involves gathering information about the client's family history, including any notable events or relationships that may have shaped their experiences. Similarly, the counselor should inquire about the client's medical history, in order to gain insight into any physical or mental health concerns that may be impacting their current state of mind.

It is also important to understand the client's educational background, as this can provide valuable context for their current situation. This includes not only the client's academic achievements, but also any experiences or challenges that they may have faced in the educational setting. Additionally, understanding the client's social and cultural context can be crucial in developing a strong therapeutic relationship.

Once the counselor has gathered information about the client's background, the next step is to inquire about their current situation. This includes asking about the client's work, relationships, and daily routines. By gaining insight into the client's day-to-day life, the counselor can better understand the challenges that they may be facing and develop strategies for addressing them in therapy.

Throughout this process, it is important for the counselor to approach the client with sensitivity and respect. Some clients may have experienced trauma or other difficult life events, and it is crucial for the counselor to create a safe and supportive environment for them to discuss these experiences. Additionally, the counselor should be aware of their own biases and assumptions, and work to avoid making judgments or assumptions about the client's experiences. By fostering an open and non-judgmental environment, the counselor can work with the client to develop effective strategies for addressing their concerns and achieving their goals.

Identifying the Client's Goals and Needs

Once the counselor has built a relationship with the client, it is important to continue to cultivate that relationship. This can involve spending more time with the client, learning more about their history and background, and understanding their unique needs and concerns. In doing so, the counselor can gain a deeper understanding of the client's situation, which can inform the development of a more effective treatment plan.

Identifying the client's goals and needs is a crucial step in this process. The counselor should work collaboratively with the client to develop a treatment plan that addresses their unique needs and concerns. This can involve encouraging the client to identify their own goals and priorities, and to express their thoughts and feelings about the counseling process. The counselor should also provide guidance and support in developing realistic and achievable goals, and in identifying the steps necessary to achieve those goals.

In addition, the counselor should be aware of the potential challenges and barriers that the client may face in achieving their goals. This can involve addressing issues such as financial constraints, social support, and access to resources. By taking a holistic approach to treatment, the counselor can help the client to navigate these challenges and to achieve their goals in a way that is sustainable and meaningful.

Overall, understanding the client is a crucial aspect of the counseling process. By building a strong therapeutic relationship, learning about the client's history and background, and identifying their goals and needs, the counselor can provide effective and individualized care that meets the client's unique needs and circumstances. By working collaboratively with the client and providing ongoing support, the counselor can help the client to achieve long-term success and a greater sense of well-being.

3.2 The Role of the Counselor

The role of the counselor in the counseling process is central to the success of therapy. Counselors are trained professionals who provide support, guidance, and expertise to clients who are experiencing a range of emotional, psychological, and behavioral challenges. The counseling process involves a collaborative and client-centered approach that is designed to empower clients to explore their thoughts and feelings, gain insight into their problems, and develop new skills and strategies for personal growth and change.

One of the key aspects of the counselor's role is to provide a safe and supportive environment for the client. This involves building a strong therapeutic relationship that is based on empathy, trust, and respect. Counselors use a range of techniques and tools to establish this relationship, including active listening, unconditional positive regard, and a non-judgmental approach. By creating a safe and secure space, counselors can help clients feel comfortable and accepted, which can facilitate the healing process.

In addition to building a strong therapeutic relationship, counselors are responsible for understanding the client's unique needs and circumstances. This involves taking a holistic and client-centered approach that considers the client's physical, emotional, social, and spiritual well-being. Counselors use a range of counseling techniques and tools to assess the client's needs and goals, including standardized assessments, clinical interviews, and self-report measures. By gathering comprehensive information about the client's life experiences, cultural background, and personal values, counselors can develop a deeper understanding of the client's challenges and strengths.

Once counselors have a clear understanding of the client's needs and goals, they work with the client to develop a treatment plan that is tailored to their unique circumstances. This treatment plan may involve a range of interventions and techniques, including cognitive-behavioral therapy, solution-focused therapy, narrative therapy, and mindfulness practices. Counselors also use spiritual interventions and resources to enhance the counseling process and outcomes. This may involve incorporating prayer, scripture, or other spiritual practices into the counseling sessions.

Throughout the counseling process, counselors are responsible for maintaining ethical and professional standards of care. This includes ensuring client confidentiality, obtaining informed consent, and adhering to the code of ethics for their profession. Counselors are also responsible for being aware of their own biases and assumptions, and working to avoid imposing their values or beliefs on the client.

Overall, the counselor's role in the counseling process is vital and multifaceted. It involves providing support, guidance, and expertise to clients who are experiencing a range of emotional, psychological, and behavioral challenges. By creating a safe and supportive environment, understanding the client's unique needs, and developing a tailored treatment plan, counselors can help clients achieve their goals, improve their well-being, and live a more fulfilling life.

3.3 The Counseling Relationship

The counseling relationship is often considered one of the most important and meaningful aspects of the counseling process. It is a unique bond that is built between the counselor and the client, based on mutual respect, trust, and empathy.

To establish a strong therapeutic alliance, it is important that the counseling relationship is collaborative and client-centered. This means that the client should be actively involved in their own care and decision-making, and the counselor should be sensitive to the client's individual needs and preferences. The counselor should work to create a safe and supportive environment where the client feels comfortable sharing their thoughts and feelings in a non-judgmental manner.

Communication is also a crucial component of the counseling relationship. It is important that the counselor communicates their role and expectations to the client in a clear and transparent manner, and provides them with regular feedback and support throughout the counseling process. The counselor should be mindful of the client's communication style and preferences, and work to adapt their approach accordingly.

Another important aspect of the counseling relationship is the establishment of clear boundaries and expectations. This involves discussing the purpose and goals of counseling, as well as the frequency and duration of sessions. The counselor should also be clear about the limits of confidentiality, and ensure that the client understands their rights and responsibilities in the counseling process. By empowering the client to participate in their own care, the counselor can help them to achieve their goals and make progress towards a more fulfilling life.

Building a strong therapeutic relationship is essential to the counseling process, as it helps to facilitate a more positive therapeutic experience and increase the likelihood of successful outcomes. By working collaboratively with the client and providing ongoing support, the counselor can help the client to achieve long-term success and a greater sense of well-being.

In addition, the counseling relationship is also important in promoting a sense of community and belonging. Through the counseling process, clients are able to connect with a caring and supportive professional who will listen and provide guidance through difficult times. This can help to reduce feelings of isolation and promote a sense of empowerment and resilience.

Overall, the counseling relationship is a unique and valuable aspect of the counseling process. By building a strong therapeutic alliance with the client, the counselor can provide effective and individualized care that meets the client's unique needs and circumstances. It is important that counselors give this aspect of counseling the attention and care that it deserves, in order to help clients achieve their goals and improve their well-being.

3.4 The Counseling Process

The counseling process is a comprehensive and well-planned approach aimed at helping clients achieve their goals, overcome challenges, and improve their overall well-being. The process involves a number of stages that are carefully designed to ensure effective treatment and successful outcomes.

Assessment, which is the first stage of the counseling process, involves gathering relevant information about the client's situation. This step is crucial in identifying the client's needs and challenges, and helps to determine the most appropriate course of action. Once the assessment is complete, the counselor will work with the client to develop a treatment plan that is tailored to their specific needs and goals.

The implementation stage is where the actual counseling sessions take place. During this stage, the counselor and client work together to put the treatment plan into action. This may involve a variety of techniques and interventions, such as talk therapy, cognitive-behavioral therapy, relaxation exercises, and more. The counselor will also provide ongoing support, guidance, and feedback to the client throughout the treatment process.

Finally, the evaluation stage is where the counselor and client assess the effectiveness of the treatment and make any necessary adjustments. This stage is crucial in ensuring that the client achieves their goals and that the treatment is successful. By carefully monitoring progress and making adjustments as needed, the counseling process can help clients achieve lasting positive change in their lives.

Assessment

The first stage of the counseling process is assessment, which is a critical step in developing a comprehensive understanding of the client's history, background, and current situation. To achieve this, the counselor may use various assessment tools, such as interviews, questionnaires, and standardized tests, to gather detailed information about the client's current situation, mental health, and goals.

Assessment is an ongoing process that involves multiple steps, including information gathering, interpretation, and synthesis. After gathering information, the counselor should analyze and interpret the data to identify patterns and potential issues that need to be addressed. This analysis can help the counselor to develop a more nuanced understanding of the client's situation and provide more targeted and effective treatment.

During the assessment process, it is essential for the counselor to create a safe and supportive environment where the client can feel comfortable sharing their thoughts and feelings. The counselor should use active listening and empathic responding to demonstrate their understanding and support. This can help to build trust and rapport with the client, which is essential for the success of the counseling relationship.

Moreover, the assessment process should be client-centered, meaning that the client should be actively involved in identifying their goals and needs. This collaborative approach can help the client to feel empowered and invested in their own treatment, which can increase their motivation and engagement.

In addition, cultural competence is critical during the assessment process. The counselor should be sensitive to the client's cultural and social context and work to avoid making assumptions or judgments about the client's experiences. This can help to prevent misunderstandings and establish a more positive therapeutic relationship.

To summarize, the assessment process is a complex and multi-faceted stage of the counseling process that requires sensitivity, collaboration, and cultural competence. By taking a client-centered and collaborative approach, the counselor can build a strong therapeutic relationship with the client and develop a more nuanced understanding of their needs and goals.

Treatment Planning

The counseling process is a multi-step journey that involves several stages. The first stage is establishing a therapeutic relationship between the counselor and the client. This is a crucial step, as it sets the foundation for the rest of the counseling process.

Once the therapeutic relationship has been established, the next stage is treatment planning. This is where the counselor and the client work together to develop a comprehensive plan that is tailored to the client's unique needs, concerns, and goals. The treatment plan should be collaborative and client-centered, meaning that the client should be an active participant in the development of their own plan.

Developing a treatment plan is not a simple task. It requires a thorough understanding of the client's history, personality, and current situation. The counselor must take into account the client's strengths and limitations, as well as any potential barriers that may hinder their progress. To do this, the counselor may need to conduct assessments, gather information from other sources, and consult with other professionals.

Once the client's needs and goals have been identified, the counselor and the client can begin to develop a plan of action. This plan should be realistic and achievable, and should be broken down into manageable steps that the client can realistically accomplish. The counselor should explain the different steps involved in the plan, and ensure that the client understands their role and responsibilities.

Throughout the treatment planning process, the counselor must provide guidance and support to the client. This includes explaining the different options available to the client, helping them to understand the potential benefits and drawbacks of each option, and providing resources and referrals as needed. The counselor should also monitor the client's progress and adjust the treatment plan as needed.

The success of the treatment plan ultimately depends on the client's willingness and ability to actively participate in the process. The counselor should work with the client to set achievable goals, provide support and encouragement along the way, and celebrate successes along the journey.

Implementation

The implementation stage of the counseling process is a critical step that requires careful attention to detail in order to put the treatment plan into action effectively. One way to achieve this is through the use of tailored interventions that take into account the unique needs and circumstances of each individual client. By creating a customized approach to therapy, the counselor can help the client see tangible progress towards their goals.

The interventions that may be used during the implementation stage can vary depending on the client's specific needs. For example, individual therapy sessions may be used to address specific issues and help the client develop coping mechanisms. In contrast, group therapy sessions may be used to promote social skills and provide a support system that encourages clients to learn from one another.

Another important consideration during the implementation stage is the potential use of medication. If the client is struggling with symptoms that are related to underlying physiological issues, medication may be prescribed to help manage these symptoms. Additionally, referrals to other healthcare providers may be made if the client requires specialized care that falls outside the scope of the counselor's expertise.

Throughout the implementation process, it is important for the counselor to work collaboratively with the client. This means that the client should be an active participant in their own care and decision-making. By fostering an environment of collaboration and trust, the counselor can help the client feel more invested in the process and more likely to follow through with the treatment plan.

To ensure that the treatment plan is effective, the counselor should monitor the client's progress throughout the implementation stage. This includes tracking their progress towards their goals, as well as monitoring any changes in their mental health or overall well-being. If necessary, adjustments to the treatment plan should be made to ensure that the client is receiving the best possible care.

Evaluation

The final stage of the counseling process is a crucial step in ensuring that the client receives the most effective care possible. During this evaluation process, the counselor assesses the client's progress and evaluates the effectiveness of the treatment plan. The counselor may use various tools such as interviews, questionnaires, and standardized tests to gather information for the evaluation process. The use of these tools allows for a more comprehensive understanding of the client's progress and helps identify areas where improvements can be made.

It is important to note that the evaluation process should be collaborative and client-centered. By involving the client in the process, the counselor empowers them to assess their own progress and identify areas where they can improve. This approach fosters a sense of ownership and responsibility in the client, which can increase their motivation to make positive changes.

Throughout the evaluation process, the counselor should provide feedback and support to the client. This support can help the client feel more confident and motivated to make positive changes. Additionally, the counselor should work with the client to identify areas of strength and build upon them. This can help the client develop a positive self-image and increase their confidence in their ability to achieve their goals.

It is worth noting that the counseling process is a structured and systematic approach to helping clients achieve their goals and improve their well-being. By using a collaborative and client-centered approach, the counselor can provide effective and individualized care that meets the client's unique needs and circumstances, and encourages them to take an active role in their own progress. By prioritizing the evaluation process, the counselor can ensure that the client is receiving the best possible care and is on track to achieve their goals.

3.5 Ethical Considerations in Christian Counseling

Ethical considerations are an important aspect of the counseling process, and are particularly important in Christian counseling. Christian counselors are held to high ethical standards, and are expected to provide care that is compassionate, competent, and respectful of the client's autonomy and rights.

Some of the key ethical considerations in Christian counseling include:

- Confidentiality: Christian counselors are required to maintain strict confidentiality in their work with clients, except under certain circumstances, such as when the client poses a danger to themselves or others. The counselor should inform the client of their rights and limitations related to confidentiality, and should respect their wishes regarding the disclosure of information.

- Informed Consent: Christian counselors are required to obtain informed consent from their clients before beginning treatment. This involves providing the client with information about the counseling process, including the purpose and goals of counseling, the limits of confidentiality, and the counselor's qualifications and experience. The counselor should ensure that the client understands their rights and responsibilities in the counseling process, and that they feel empowered to participate in their own care.
- Competence: Christian counselors are required to provide care that is competent and based on the latest research and techniques in the field of counseling. They should also be aware of their own limitations and seek consultation or referral when necessary.
- Boundaries: Christian counselors are required to establish clear and appropriate boundaries with their clients, and to avoid dual relationships or conflicts of interest that may compromise the counseling relationship.
- Cultural Sensitivity: Christian counselors are required to be sensitive to the client's cultural and social context, and to avoid making assumptions or judgments about their experiences. They should also work to develop cultural competence and awareness, and to provide care that is respectful and sensitive to the client's unique needs and circumstances.
- Non-Discrimination: Christian counselors are required to provide care that is free from discrimination or prejudice based on factors such as race, ethnicity, gender, sexual orientation, religion, or disability. They should strive to provide care that is inclusive and welcoming to all clients, regardless of their background or identity.
- Professionalism: Christian counselors are required to maintain a high level of professionalism in their work, and to adhere to ethical and legal standards in the field

of counseling. They should also engage in ongoing professional development and self-reflection to improve their practice.

- Supervision: Christian counselors are required to seek supervision and consultation from qualified professionals in the field of counseling, in order to ensure that they are providing competent and effective care. They should also be open to feedback and constructive criticism, and use this feedback to improve their practice.
- Referral: Christian counselors are required to refer clients to other qualified professionals when necessary, such as when the client requires specialized care or treatment that is outside the counselor's scope of practice. They should also provide appropriate follow-up and support to the client during the referral process.
- Spiritual Integration: Christian counselors are required to integrate faith and spirituality into the counseling process in a way that is respectful and appropriate to the client's beliefs and values. They should be aware of the client's spiritual needs and desires, and be prepared to offer spiritual interventions and resources when appropriate.
- Self-Care: Christian counselors are required to engage in self-care practices that promote their own physical, emotional, and spiritual health and well-being. They should also be aware of the risk of burnout and compassion fatigue in the counseling profession, and take steps to prevent and address these issues.

In summary, ethical considerations are a crucial aspect of the counseling process, and are particularly important in Christian counseling. Christian counselors are held to high ethical standards, and are expected to provide care that is compassionate, competent, and respectful of the client's autonomy and rights. By following these ethical guidelines,

Christian counselors can provide effective and ethical care that meets the client's unique needs and circumstances.

Chapter 4: Specific Issues in Christian Counseling

4.1 Marriage and Family Counseling

Marriage and Family Counseling

Marriage and family counseling is a highly specialized area of counseling that focuses on providing guidance, support, and effective strategies to couples and families in order to help them navigate through various challenges and develop healthy and fulfilling relationships that stand the test of time.

The process of marriage and family counseling is designed to provide couples and families with the tools they need to overcome common obstacles such as communication difficulties, conflicts, financial issues, or other problems that may be impacting their relationships. By working with a skilled and experienced counselor, couples and families can gain a deeper understanding of their unique needs and learn how to develop healthier and more effective ways of relating to one another.

In addition to addressing immediate concerns, marriage and family counseling can also help to prevent future issues from arising, by teaching couples and families valuable skills and techniques for maintaining positive and healthy relationships. Whether you are looking to improve communication, resolve conflicts, or simply strengthen your bond with your partner or family members, marriage and family counseling can provide you with the support, guidance, and resources you need to achieve your goals.

The Role of the Counselor

In marriage counseling, the counselor's role is to help the couple identify the underlying issues that are causing conflict or tension in the relationship. Some couples may struggle with communication or trust, while others may have different expectations for their partner. The counselor should work with the couple to explore these issues in depth and develop strategies to address them.

To create a safe and supportive environment for the couple, the counselor should establish trust and rapport with both partners. This may involve actively listening to their concerns, validating their emotions, and refraining from judgment or criticism. In addition, the counselor may use techniques such as mirroring or paraphrasing to help the couple better understand each other's perspectives.

Similarly, in family counseling, the counselor's role is to help the family identify and address issues that are impacting their functioning. These issues may include communication difficulties, conflict, or individual behaviors that are causing tension in the family. The counselor should work with the family as a unit to explore these issues and develop strategies to improve the family's overall functioning.

To create a safe and supportive environment for all family members, the counselor should establish a sense of trust and respect with each individual. This may involve actively listening to each person's concerns, validating their emotions, and refraining from judgment or criticism. The counselor may also use techniques such as role-playing or family sculpting to help the family members better understand each other's perspectives and improve their communication skills.

Techniques and Approaches

Marriage and family counseling can involve a range of techniques and approaches to address the specific needs of the couple or family. Some of these techniques and approaches may include:

- Cognitive-behavioral therapy (CBT): This approach helps individuals identify and modify negative thinking patterns and behaviors that contribute to their symptoms. It also empowers individuals to take control of their thoughts and feelings, and to develop coping strategies for managing stress and anxiety.
- Emotionally-focused therapy (EFT): This approach focuses on the emotional bonds between individuals and helps them develop healthier and more meaningful relationships. The goal is to help individuals express their emotions in a more productive way and to build stronger connections with each other.
- Narrative therapy: This approach helps individuals explore their personal stories and how these stories shape their beliefs and behaviors. By understanding their own stories, individuals can gain insight into their problems and develop new perspectives on their lives.
- Solution-focused therapy: This approach focuses on helping individuals identify and achieve their goals. It emphasizes the strengths and resources of the individual and encourages them to build on these strengths to achieve success.

Marriage and family counseling can be a powerful tool in building stronger relationships between couples and family members. When combined with faith-based interventions and resources, counseling can be even more effective in providing long-lasting solutions to relationship issues. By incorporating prayer, scripture, or other spiritual practices into the counseling process, counselors can help clients develop a deeper understanding of their faith and how it can guide their relationships. This can lead to a more meaningful and fulfilling relationship with God, and provide a sense of purpose and direction during difficult times. Additionally, faith-based interventions can help clients find comfort and hope in their relationship with God, and provide a source of strength and resilience when facing relationship challenges. By working with the couple or family to integrate these spiritual practices and resources into the counseling process, counselors can help clients achieve lasting change and growth in their relationships.

Examples

- Communication difficulties
- Conflict resolution
- Infidelity
- Parenting challenges
- Blended family issues
- Financial stress
- Mental health concerns
- Substance abuse
- Domestic violence

Marriage and family counseling is a valuable resource that can help individuals in various ways. It is a powerful tool that allows individuals to work through challenges and improve their relationships. The counseling process provides a safe and supportive environment where individuals can explore their thoughts and feelings. In this way, they can gain insight into their problems, develop new skills, and learn new strategies for personal growth and change.

Additionally, marriage and family counseling can also incorporate faith-based interventions. These interventions can provide individuals with the guidance and support they need to build stronger and more fulfilling relationships with their partners and family members. By working with a skilled counselor, individuals can gain the tools they need to navigate life's challenges and improve their emotional well-being. Overall, marriage and family counseling is an excellent resource for anyone looking to improve their relationships and overcome personal obstacles.

4.2 Grief and Loss Counseling

Grief and loss can be incredibly challenging to cope with, and it's normal to feel a sense of isolation and confusion during these times. It's important to acknowledge that everyone experiences grief in their own unique way, and there is no "right" or "wrong" way to grieve. That being said, there are a multitude of resources available to help individuals and families navigate the complex process of grieving and adjusting to significant life changes.

One of the most effective resources available is grief counseling. This type of counseling is specifically designed to help individuals and families process their emotions and feelings in a safe and supportive environment. A trained professional can help individuals and families gain a deeper understanding of their own unique experiences with grief, and provide them with the tools and resources they need to heal and move forward in a healthy way.

Grief counseling can offer a safe and non-judgmental space to express emotions, process feelings, and learn coping strategies. It's important to understand that grief is a complex and ongoing process, and it may take time to find a sense of peace and acceptance. However, with the right support, individuals and families can begin to heal and move forward in a positive direction.

In addition to grief counseling, there are many other resources available to help individuals and families cope with loss and navigate significant life changes. These resources include support groups, online forums, and self-help books. It's important to explore all of the available resources and find the ones that work best for your individual needs and circumstances.

Remember, grief is a natural and normal part of the human experience, and it's okay to seek help and support during these challenging times. With the right resources and support, individuals and families can find hope and healing in the midst of loss and change.

Understanding Grief and Loss

Losing a loved one is an incredibly challenging experience that can have significant impacts on a person's emotional and physical wellbeing. It's normal to feel grief after losing someone important to us. The grief process can manifest in many ways, including feelings of sadness, anger, guilt, confusion, and even physical symptoms like fatigue or loss of appetite.

The journey of grief is often long and complex, and there are many ways to cope with the difficult emotions that come with it. Some people find solace in talking to friends and family members about their feelings, while others turn to spiritual or religious practices for support. Engaging in physical exercise, meditation, or other stress-reducing activities can also be helpful in managing the overwhelming emotions that come with grief.

It's important to remember that everyone experiences grief differently, and there is no "right" way to navigate the process. The most important thing is to be gentle with yourself and to allow yourself time and space to grieve in your own way. While it may be tempting to try to push through the pain and move on quickly, it's important to honor the process and allow yourself to fully experience the emotions that come with losing someone you love. In time, with patience and self-compassion, it is possible to find a sense of peace and acceptance after a loss.

The Value of Grief Counseling

Grief is a complex and difficult emotion that can be hard to manage alone. It can manifest in different ways and affect individuals in unique ways. Grief counseling is a valuable resource for those individuals who are struggling with grief and loss, as it can provide them with the support, guidance, and practical strategies they need to cope with the challenges of grief.

Grief counselors are trained professionals who can help individuals navigate the various stages of grief, from initial shock and denial to eventual acceptance and healing. They can offer a safe and supportive space for individuals to express their feelings, thoughts, and concerns, and help them develop the skills and tools they need to work through their grief in a healthy and productive way.

In addition to providing emotional support, grief counselors can also offer practical advice and information on how to deal with the practical aspects of grief, such as managing funeral arrangements, dealing with legal and financial issues, and coping with the stress and strain of daily life while grieving. They can also provide referrals to other professionals or support groups, as needed, to ensure that individuals get the comprehensive support they need to navigate the complex and challenging journey of grief. Overall, grief counseling can be an essential resource for anyone struggling with the profound pain and loss that comes with grief, helping them find a sense of hope, healing, and renewal in the midst of their sorrow.

The Role of the Grief Counselor

Grief counseling is a process that focuses on helping a client work through their emotions and feelings of loss. The primary role of the counselor is to provide support and guidance as the client navigates through the many different emotions and stages of grief that may arise after a loss. By helping the client identify and acknowledge their emotions, the counselor can begin to develop strategies to help the client cope with their grief.

One of the most important aspects of grief counseling is helping clients explore different coping mechanisms. This may involve mindfulness practices, journaling, or creative expression. By encouraging clients to try a variety of coping mechanisms, the counselor can help them find the techniques that work best for them. Additionally, the counselor can provide support and guidance as the client navigates through the various stages of grief.

The stages of grief are numerous and can be difficult to navigate. The counselor can assist the client in recognizing and working through each stage, which may include shock, denial, anger, bargaining, depression, and acceptance. By working through these stages, the client can begin to find a sense of closure and meaning in their loss, leading to a healthier and more positive outlook on the future.

Christian Grief Counseling

Christian grief counseling is a specialized form of counseling that provides support and guidance to individuals who are experiencing grief and loss from a Christian perspective. It not only considers the psychological and emotional aspects of the grieving process but also incorporates faith-based interventions and resources into the counseling process.

In Christian grief counseling, counselors may work with clients to explore their spiritual beliefs and practices, and help them develop a deeper understanding of their faith and its role in their grieving process. Counselors may also encourage clients to find comfort and solace in prayer, scripture, or other spiritual practices.

By integrating faith and spirituality into the counseling process, Christian grief counselors provide a unique perspective and approach to grief counseling that can be especially meaningful for individuals who find comfort and healing in their relationship with God. With this approach, clients can find not only emotional and psychological support but also spiritual comfort and strength to help them navigate the difficult process of grief.

How Grief and Loss Counseling Works

Examples of how grief and loss counseling works may include the following:

- Providing a safe and supportive environment for clients to express their feelings and thoughts about their loss
- Helping clients to identify and acknowledge their emotions, and to express them in healthy ways
- Teaching clients coping strategies, such as mindfulness, deep breathing, or visualization techniques, to help them manage their emotions and reduce stress
- Encouraging clients to engage in self-care activities, such as exercise, healthy eating, and restful sleep, to promote physical and emotional well-being
- Exploring the client's spiritual beliefs and practices, and incorporating them into the counseling process if appropriate
- Providing education about the different stages of grief, and helping clients to recognize where they are in the grieving process
- Encouraging clients to set goals and work towards a sense of closure and meaning in their loss
- Providing support and guidance to help clients navigate the practical challenges of grief, such as dealing with legal and financial issues, or making funeral arrangements

Conclusion

In conclusion, it is important to recognize that grief and loss can be a difficult and challenging experience for individuals. Whether it is the loss of a loved one, a significant life change, or any other form of loss, the feelings of sadness, confusion, and even anger can be overwhelming. Fortunately, there are resources available to help individuals navigate through their grief, and one of the most valuable resources is grief and loss counseling.

In counseling sessions, individuals can work with a trained professional who can provide support, guidance, and practical strategies to help them cope with their grief. Counselors can help individuals understand their emotions, develop coping skills, and find ways to move forward after a loss. Additionally, counseling can provide individuals with a safe and non-judgmental space to express their feelings and work through their grief.

By working with a grief counselor, individuals can find a sense of closure, meaning, and healing in their loss. They can learn to accept their feelings and work through them in a healthy way, which can lead to a greater sense of well-being and peace. Furthermore, the skills and strategies learned in counseling can be applied to other areas of life, helping individuals to better navigate through future challenges.

In summary, while grief and loss can be a difficult and painful experience, it is important to remember that help is available. Grief and loss counseling can provide the support, guidance, and practical strategies needed to navigate through the challenges of grief, and can ultimately lead to a sense of closure, meaning, and healing.

4.3 Addiction Counseling

Addiction counseling is an incredibly important field that requires a great deal of skill and expertise. It is a specialized area of counseling that focuses on helping individuals overcome substance abuse and other addictive behaviors, but it is also much more than that. Addiction counselors work with their clients to help them understand the underlying causes of their addiction and develop coping strategies to deal with these issues in a healthy and productive way.

One of the key aspects of addiction counseling is that it is a collaborative process. Counselors work closely with their clients to develop individualized treatment plans that are tailored to their specific needs and goals. This may involve a combination of individual therapy, group therapy, and other types of support, depending on the client's needs.

Another important aspect of addiction counseling is that it is a holistic approach. Counselors take into account not just the individual's addiction, but also their physical, emotional, and social well-being. This means that addiction counselors may work with other healthcare professionals, such as doctors and nutritionists, to ensure that their clients are receiving a comprehensive approach to their treatment.

Overall, addiction counseling is a vital component of the recovery process for individuals who are struggling with addiction. It provides a safe and supportive environment where individuals can explore their feelings and experiences, develop new coping strategies, and work towards a healthier and happier future.

The Addiction Counseling Process

The addiction counseling process is a collaborative effort between the counselor and the client. This partnership begins with an assessment, which is a critical step that helps the counselor understand the client's unique situation. During the assessment phase, the counselor may ask questions about the client's background, including their family history and any past experiences with addiction. The counselor may also assess the client's mental health status, including any underlying conditions that may be contributing to their substance abuse. In addition, the counselor may gather information on the client's social and environmental factors that may be affecting their addiction, such as peer pressure or job-related stress.

Once the assessment is complete, the counselor uses this information to develop a customized treatment plan that is tailored to the client's specific needs. The treatment plan may include a range of interventions, such as individual therapy, group therapy, family therapy, and medication management. The counselor and client work together throughout the counseling process, regularly evaluating the effectiveness of the treatment plan and making adjustments as necessary. This ongoing collaboration is essential to ensure that the client is getting the support they need to overcome their addiction.

Furthermore, the counselor provides ongoing support and education to the client, helping them to develop the skills and tools they need for long-term recovery. This support may include teaching the client coping mechanisms to deal with stress and cravings, as well as providing guidance on how to rebuild relationships that may have been damaged during their addiction. The counselor may also work with the client to develop a relapse prevention plan, which outlines strategies to avoid triggers and stay on track with their recovery goals.

In summary, the addiction counseling process is a comprehensive and collaborative effort between the counselor and the client. By working together to assess the client's unique situation, develop a tailored treatment plan, and provide ongoing support and education, the counselor helps the client to achieve long-term recovery from their addiction.

One of the primary goals of addiction counseling is to help clients identify and address the underlying issues that contribute to their addiction. These issues may include trauma, stress, anxiety, depression, or other mental health conditions. It is important to recognize that addiction is often a symptom of a larger problem, and that addressing the underlying issues is critical to achieving lasting recovery.

In addition to addressing these underlying issues, addiction counseling also focuses on helping clients develop the skills they need to maintain their sobriety after they leave counseling. This may involve developing strategies for managing cravings and triggers, improving communication and relationship skills, and building a support network of family, friends, and other individuals who can provide encouragement and accountability.

Furthermore, addiction counseling can also assist clients in setting and achieving personal and professional goals. By working with a counselor, clients can identify areas of their lives that they want to improve, and develop a plan to achieve those goals. This can include anything from finding a new job or improving their financial situation, to pursuing hobbies and interests that they may have neglected during their addiction.

Ultimately, addiction counseling is a collaborative process between the client and the counselor. Through this process, clients can gain a better understanding of their addiction and the underlying issues that contribute to it, develop the skills they need to maintain their sobriety, and achieve their personal and professional goals.

Christian Addiction Counseling

Christian addiction counseling takes a faith-based approach to addiction recovery. It incorporates Christian principles and beliefs into the counseling process, helping clients develop a deeper understanding of their faith and its role in their recovery. Christian addiction counselors may incorporate prayer, scripture, or other spiritual practices into the counseling sessions, helping clients connect with God and find comfort and strength in their faith.

Examples of Christian addiction counseling techniques include:

- Exploring the client's spiritual journey and relationship with God
- Incorporating prayer, meditation, or other spiritual practices into the counseling sessions
- Encouraging clients to attend church or participate in Christian fellowship groups
- Helping clients develop a deeper understanding of their identity in Christ
- Using biblical stories or parables to illustrate key principles of addiction recovery
- Incorporating forgiveness and grace into the counseling process
- Encouraging clients to develop a personal relationship with God

Overall, addiction counseling is an essential part of the addiction recovery process. Christian addiction counseling takes a faith-based approach to addiction recovery, incorporating Christian principles and beliefs into the counseling process. By addressing the underlying issues that contribute to addiction and helping clients develop the skills they need to maintain their sobriety, addiction counselors can provide a path to lasting recovery and healing.

4.4 Depression and Anxiety Counseling

Understanding Depression and Anxiety Counseling

Depression and anxiety counseling is a form of therapy that helps individuals manage and cope with symptoms of depression and anxiety. These mental health conditions can be debilitating and impact all areas of a person's life, from work to relationships. Counseling can provide individuals with the tools and support they need to better manage their symptoms and improve their overall mental health.

Goals of Depression and Anxiety Counseling

The primary goal of depression and anxiety counseling is to help individuals better understand their symptoms and develop strategies for managing them. Some common goals of depression and anxiety counseling include:

- Identifying the root causes of depression or anxiety
- Developing coping strategies for managing symptoms
- Improving communication and interpersonal relationships
- Addressing negative thought patterns and behaviors
- Improving self-esteem and self-confidence
- Enhancing overall mental health and well-being

Methods Used in Depression and Anxiety Counseling

Depression and anxiety counseling may involve a range of therapeutic approaches, depending on the needs and preferences of the individual. Some common methods used in depression and anxiety counseling include:

- Cognitive-behavioral therapy (CBT)
- Dialectical behavior therapy (DBT)
- Mindfulness-based therapy
- Acceptance and commitment therapy (ACT)
- Psychodynamic therapy
- Solution-focused brief therapy (SFBT)

Incorporating Faith-Based Approaches in Depression and Anxiety Counseling

For individuals who value their faith, incorporating faith-based approaches in depression and anxiety counseling can be a valuable tool for promoting healing and growth. Some ways in which faith-based approaches may be incorporated include:

- Exploring the role of spirituality in mental health
- Incorporating prayer or other spiritual practices into counseling sessions
- Using scripture or other religious texts to guide the counseling process
- Encouraging individuals to connect with their faith community for additional support

Examples of Coping Strategies for Depression and Anxiety

One of the key goals of depression and anxiety counseling is to help individuals develop coping strategies for managing their symptoms. Here are some examples of coping strategies that may be helpful:

- Practicing mindfulness meditation
- Engaging in regular physical exercise
- Prioritizing self-care activities, such as taking a bath or reading a book
- Keeping a journal to track moods and emotions
- Using relaxation techniques, such as deep breathing or progressive muscle relaxation
- Setting small, achievable goals and celebrating successes
- Practicing positive self-talk and challenging negative thoughts
- Seeking support from loved ones or a support group
- Seeking professional help when needed, such as medication or therapy

By working with a counselor and utilizing these coping strategies, individuals can better manage their symptoms of depression and anxiety and improve their overall mental health and well-being.

4.5 Trauma and Abuse Counseling

Understanding Trauma and Abuse Counseling

Trauma and abuse counseling is a type of therapy that helps individuals recover from traumatic experiences and abuse. Trauma can refer to any event or experience that causes significant emotional distress or a threat to one's physical safety, while abuse refers to any behavior that is meant to control or harm another person. Trauma and abuse can have long-lasting impacts on an individual's mental health and well-being, and counseling can provide individuals with the tools and support they need to heal and recover.

Goals of Trauma and Abuse Counseling

The primary goal of trauma and abuse counseling is to help individuals heal from the emotional and psychological impact of traumatic experiences and abuse. Some common goals of trauma and abuse counseling include:

- Processing and working through the traumatic event or abuse
- Developing coping strategies for managing symptoms of post-traumatic stress disorder (PTSD) and anxiety
- Addressing any negative thought patterns or beliefs that may be holding the individual back
- Building resilience and improving overall mental health and well-being
- Encouraging healthy boundaries and relationships

Methods Used in Trauma and Abuse Counseling

Trauma and abuse counseling may involve a range of therapeutic approaches, depending on the needs and preferences of the individual. Some common methods used in trauma and abuse counseling include:

- Cognitive-behavioral therapy (CBT)
- Eye Movement Desensitization and Reprocessing (EMDR)
- Psychodynamic therapy
- Dialectical behavior therapy (DBT)
- Somatic experiencing therapy
- Narrative therapy

Incorporating Faith-Based Approaches in Trauma and Abuse Counseling

For individuals who value their faith, incorporating faith-based approaches in trauma and abuse counseling can be a valuable tool for promoting healing and growth. Some ways in which faith-based approaches may be incorporated include:

- Exploring the role of spirituality in healing from trauma and abuse
- Incorporating prayer or other spiritual practices into counseling sessions
- Using scripture or other religious texts to guide the counseling process
- Encouraging individuals to connect with their faith community for additional support

Types of Trauma and Abuse

Trauma and abuse can take many forms, and it's important to understand the different types of trauma and abuse that individuals may experience. Some common types of trauma and abuse include:

- Physical abuse, such as hitting or punching
- Sexual abuse, such as unwanted sexual contact or assault
- Emotional abuse, such as belittling or gaslighting
- Neglect, such as failing to provide basic needs like food, clothing, or shelter
- Domestic violence, which includes physical, emotional, and sexual abuse within intimate relationships
- Childhood trauma, which can include abuse, neglect, or other traumatic experiences that occurred during childhood

One of the key goals of trauma and abuse counseling is to help individuals develop coping strategies for managing their symptoms and improving their mental health. Here are some examples of coping strategies that may be helpful:

- Engaging in relaxation techniques, such as deep breathing or progressive muscle relaxation
- Practicing mindfulness meditation
- Setting boundaries with individuals who may be triggering or harmful
- Seeking support from loved ones or a support group
- Participating in self-care activities, such as taking a warm bath or reading a book
- Seeking professional help, such as medication or therapy
- Challenging negative thoughts and beliefs about oneself
- Developing a positive support system
- Journaling or other forms of self-expression

By working with a counselor and utilizing these coping strategies, individuals can better manage their symptoms and work towards healing and recovery from trauma and abuse.

4.6 Spiritual Direction and Formation

Benefits of Spiritual Direction and Formation Counseling

Spiritual direction and formation counseling offers numerous benefits to individuals seeking to deepen their spiritual lives and connect with their faith on a more meaningful level. Here are some of the benefits of this specialized form of counseling:

Deeper Spiritual Connection

One of the primary benefits of spiritual direction and formation counseling is that it helps individuals to deepen their spiritual connection. Through this type of counseling, clients may explore different spiritual practices and beliefs that resonate with them and incorporate them into their daily lives. This can help individuals to feel more connected to their faith and to experience a greater sense of purpose and meaning in their lives.

Increased Self-Awareness

Spiritual direction and formation counseling can also help individuals to develop a deeper understanding of themselves and their spiritual journey. By exploring their beliefs, values, and practices, clients may gain insights into their own strengths, weaknesses, and areas for growth. This increased self-awareness can help individuals to make more intentional choices and to live more fulfilling lives.

Improved Mental Health

Spiritual direction and formation counseling can also be beneficial for individuals struggling with mental health issues such as anxiety or depression. Through this type of counseling, clients may learn to rely on their faith as a source of comfort and support during difficult times. Additionally, exploring spiritual practices such as meditation or prayer can help to reduce stress and improve overall mental health.

Supportive Community

Spiritual direction and formation counseling can also provide individuals with a supportive community of like-minded individuals who share their faith and values. This can be especially helpful for individuals who may feel isolated or disconnected from their faith communities. Through this type of counseling, clients may develop new relationships and find a sense of belonging and connection.

Types of Spiritual Direction and Formation Counseling

There are several different types of spiritual direction and formation counseling, each of which may be tailored to meet the unique needs of the client. Some of the most common types of spiritual direction and formation counseling include:

Ignatian Spirituality

Ignatian spirituality is a type of spiritual direction and formation that is based on the teachings of Saint Ignatius of Loyola, the founder of the Jesuits. This type of counseling may involve exploring the Spiritual Exercises of Saint Ignatius and incorporating them into the client's daily routine.

Contemplative Prayer

Contemplative prayer is a type of spiritual direction and formation that focuses on silence and stillness as a means of deepening one's spiritual connection. This type of counseling may involve exploring different contemplative practices, such as centering prayer or lectio divina.

Mystical Spirituality

Mystical spirituality is a type of spiritual direction and formation that emphasizes the mystical experience of the divine. This type of counseling may involve exploring the works of Christian mystics such as Julian of Norwich or Teresa of Avila, and incorporating their teachings into the client's spiritual practice.

Interfaith Spirituality

Interfaith spirituality is a type of spiritual direction and formation that acknowledges and respects the diversity of different faith traditions. This type of counseling may involve exploring different religious practices and beliefs, and helping the client to find common ground between their own faith and the beliefs of others.

Examples of Spiritual Direction and Formation Counseling Techniques

Here are some examples of spiritual direction and formation counseling techniques that may be used to help individuals deepen their spiritual connection and achieve their goals:

Guided Meditation

Guided meditation is a type of spiritual practice that involves using imagery and visualization to help individuals to connect with their inner selves and to achieve a state of relaxation and mindfulness. This technique may be used in spiritual direction and formation counseling to help individuals to explore different spiritual themes or to connect with a sense of inner peace.

Techniques and Strategies in Spiritual Direction and Formation

Spiritual direction and formation may involve a variety of techniques and strategies to help individuals deepen their spiritual lives and connect with their faith. Some of the techniques and strategies that may be used include:

1. Prayer and Meditation - Prayer and meditation are essential practices in spiritual direction and formation. They can help individuals quiet their minds and connect with their inner selves and God.
2. Scripture Study - The study of sacred texts, such as the Bible or other religious texts, can help individuals gain a deeper understanding of their faith and the teachings of their religion.
3. Spiritual Exercises - Spiritual exercises are practices that help individuals cultivate specific spiritual qualities, such as compassion, forgiveness, or gratitude. Examples of spiritual exercises include practicing forgiveness meditation, developing a daily gratitude practice, or engaging in acts of service.
4. Contemplation - Contemplation is a type of meditation that involves focusing on a specific spiritual question or idea. It can help individuals gain a deeper understanding of their faith and their place in the world.
5. Journaling - Journaling can be a powerful tool in spiritual direction and formation. It allows individuals to reflect on their spiritual journey, identify areas of growth and development, and document their progress over time.

Benefits of Spiritual Direction and Formation

There are numerous benefits to participating in spiritual direction and formation, including:

1. Increased self-awareness - Spiritual direction and formation can help individuals gain a deeper understanding of their own beliefs, values, and spiritual practices.
2. Enhanced spiritual growth - By exploring their spirituality in a supportive and non-judgmental environment, individuals can develop a stronger connection to their faith and discover new ways to live out their values in the world around them.
3. Improved well-being - Spiritual direction and formation can help individuals cultivate a greater sense of inner peace, joy, and fulfillment in their lives.
4. Increased sense of purpose - By exploring their spiritual journey and discovering their purpose in life, individuals can develop a greater sense of meaning and direction in their lives.

Overall, spiritual direction and formation is a powerful tool for anyone seeking to deepen their spiritual lives and connect with their faith on a more meaningful level. By exploring their spirituality in a safe and supportive environment, individuals can develop a deeper sense of purpose, well-being, and fulfillment in their lives.

Chapter 5: Special Populations in Christian Counseling

5.1 Counseling Children and Adolescents

Counseling children and adolescents requires a unique set of skills and techniques. These young clients may have difficulty expressing their thoughts and emotions, and may be more likely to act out or engage in risky behaviors. Christian counselors who work with children and adolescents must be able to create a safe and supportive environment where clients can explore their feelings and work towards healing.

Creating a Safe and Supportive Environment:

Children and adolescents need a safe and supportive environment to feel comfortable sharing their thoughts and feelings. Christian counselors can create this environment in several ways, such as:

- Building trust: Counselors should take time to build trust with their clients, which can be done through active listening, empathy, and consistency in their approach.
- Providing a non-judgmental space: Clients should feel free to express themselves without fear of judgment or punishment. Counselors can provide this space by using open-ended questions, acknowledging their clients' feelings, and creating a warm and welcoming atmosphere.
- Understanding developmental stages: Counselors should be knowledgeable about the developmental stages of children and adolescents and tailor their approach accordingly. This includes being aware of age-appropriate language and activities, as well as understanding the unique challenges that each age group may face.

Christian counselors who work with children and adolescents can use a variety of techniques to help their clients explore their feelings and work towards healing. Some of these techniques include:

- Play therapy: This approach involves using play as a way for clients to communicate and process their emotions. For example, a child who has experienced trauma may use dolls or puppets to act out the event in a safe and controlled environment.
- Art therapy: This approach involves using art as a way for clients to express their emotions and explore their experiences. For example, a teenager who is struggling with depression may create a painting that reflects their feelings of sadness and hopelessness.
- Cognitive-behavioral therapy (CBT): This approach helps clients identify and change negative thought patterns that may be contributing to their problems. For example, a child who is struggling with anxiety may learn to recognize when their thoughts are unrealistic or irrational and replace them with more positive and realistic thoughts.
- Family therapy: This approach involves working with the client's family to address issues and promote healing. For example, a teenager who is struggling with substance abuse may benefit from family therapy to help address family dynamics that may be contributing to their behavior.
- Mindfulness techniques: These techniques involve teaching clients to be present in the moment and to manage stress and anxiety through relaxation and breathing exercises. For example, a child who is struggling with anxiety may benefit from learning deep breathing exercises to help calm their body and mind.

Christian counselors who work with children and adolescents can also incorporate biblical principles and teachings into their counseling sessions. Some examples of how this can be done include:

- Praying with clients: Counselors can pray with their clients to help them feel supported and connected to God. This can also help clients feel more comfortable sharing their thoughts and feelings.
- Using scripture: Counselors can use relevant scripture passages to help clients connect their experiences to biblical teachings. For example, a teenager who is struggling with peer pressure may benefit from learning about the biblical principle of resisting temptation.
- Fostering spiritual growth: Counselors can help clients grow in their faith by encouraging them to read the Bible, attend church, and participate in other spiritual practices that align with their beliefs and values.

Conclusion:

Counseling children and adolescents can be both challenging and rewarding. As a Christian counselor, you must have a deep understanding of the developmental stages of children and adolescents, as well as the unique challenges they face. In order to create a safe and supportive environment for your young clients, you may need to incorporate a variety of techniques, such as play therapy or art therapy. It is important to remember to use age-appropriate techniques that will engage your clients and help them feel comfortable sharing their thoughts and feelings.

In addition to these techniques, Christian counselors who work with young clients must also be able to incorporate biblical principles and teachings. This can include helping children and adolescents understand the importance of forgiveness, showing them how to apply biblical principles to their daily lives, and encouraging them to develop a personal relationship with God. By incorporating these principles into your counseling sessions, you can help your young clients grow in their faith and develop a deeper understanding of God's love and grace.

5.2 Counseling the Elderly

Introduction:

As people age, they may face a variety of challenges, including physical limitations, chronic health conditions, and social isolation. For Christian counselors who work with the elderly, it is important to provide both emotional and spiritual support. This can involve using specific techniques that address the unique needs and issues facing older adults.

Techniques for Counseling the Elderly:

1. Reminiscence Therapy: Reminiscence therapy involves encouraging elderly clients to recall positive memories and experiences from their lives. This technique can be effective in promoting well-being and reducing feelings of isolation or loneliness. Some ways to incorporate reminiscence therapy into counseling sessions include:
   - Asking clients to share stories about their childhood or young adulthood
   - Using photographs or other visual aids to stimulate memories

- o Encouraging clients to write down their memories in a journal
2. Life Review: Life review is a technique that involves helping elderly clients reflect on their life experiences and find meaning in their lives. This can be especially important for clients who may be facing the end of their lives. Some ways to incorporate life review into counseling sessions include:
    - o Encouraging clients to write an autobiography or personal history
    - o Asking clients to reflect on their accomplishments and goals
    - o Helping clients identify the important relationships and connections in their lives
3. Mindfulness Techniques: Mindfulness techniques can be helpful for elderly clients who are dealing with stress, anxiety, or other emotional issues. Some mindfulness techniques that may be effective include:
    - o Deep breathing exercises
    - o Visualization or guided imagery
    - o Progressive muscle relaxation
4. Spiritual Counseling: For Christian counselors, spiritual counseling can be an important part of working with elderly clients. This may involve helping clients connect with their faith, find comfort in their spiritual beliefs, and address any spiritual concerns or questions they may have. Some ways to incorporate spiritual counseling into counseling sessions include:
    - o Encouraging clients to pray or meditate
    - o Using scripture or other religious texts as a source of comfort and guidance
    - o Helping clients explore their beliefs and values

Challenges Facing Elderly Clients:

1. Loss of Independence: As people age, they may experience a loss of independence due to physical

limitations or health issues. This can be difficult for many elderly clients and may lead to feelings of frustration, depression, and anxiety. Christian counselors who work with elderly clients can help them address these feelings by:

- o Encouraging clients to focus on what they are still able to do, rather than what they have lost
- o Identifying ways to help clients maintain their independence and autonomy
- o Offering emotional support and encouragement

2. Bereavement: Many elderly clients have experienced the loss of loved ones, whether it be a spouse, child, or friend. This can be a challenging and emotional experience that may impact the client's mental and emotional health. Christian counselors can help clients who are grieving by:

- o Encouraging them to express their feelings and emotions
- o Helping them find ways to remember and honor their loved ones
- o Providing spiritual support and guidance

Conclusion:

Counseling elderly clients as a Christian counselor can involve a variety of techniques and approaches. By using techniques such as reminiscence therapy, life review, mindfulness, and spiritual counseling, Christian counselors can provide both emotional and spiritual support to elderly clients. It is also important to be aware of the unique challenges facing elderly clients, such as loss of independence and bereavement, and provide appropriate support and guidance to help them navigate these challenges.

5.3 Counseling People with Disabilities

People with disabilities may face a wide range of challenges, including physical limitations, social isolation, discrimination, and psychological distress. As a Christian counselor, it is essential to provide emotional and spiritual support to people with disabilities while also addressing the unique issues they face. This chapter outlines some techniques and approaches that Christian counselors can use to effectively work with people with disabilities.

1. Understanding Disability To work effectively with people with disabilities, it is important to first understand the nature of disability. Disability is not just a physical condition; it can affect a person's social, emotional, and spiritual well-being. As such, Christian counselors must have a holistic approach that takes into account the whole person and not just their physical limitations.

2. Empowerment-based Counseling Empowerment-based counseling is an approach that focuses on helping people with disabilities build their self-esteem, assertiveness, and independence. This type of counseling can be especially beneficial for clients who have experienced discrimination or social isolation. Counselors can use a variety of techniques such as affirmations, goal-setting, and role-playing to help clients feel more confident and empowered.

3. Mindfulness Techniques Mindfulness techniques can be helpful for people with disabilities who experience stress and anxiety. These techniques can include deep breathing exercises, visualization, and meditation. Counselors can teach clients how to use these techniques to manage their emotions and promote relaxation.

4. Cognitive-Behavioral Therapy Cognitive-behavioral therapy (CBT) is a technique that can help clients identify and change negative thought patterns. CBT can be especially useful for clients with disabilities who may have negative beliefs about themselves or their abilities. Christian counselors can help clients challenge these negative beliefs and develop more positive and realistic self-talk.
5. Family Therapy Family therapy can be beneficial for clients with disabilities and their families. Counselors can work with the client's family to identify and address issues that may be contributing to the client's distress. Family therapy can also help families build stronger relationships and improve communication.
6. Spiritual Counseling Spiritual counseling can be an important part of counseling for people with disabilities. Counselors can help clients connect with their faith and find comfort in their spiritual beliefs. This can include prayer, meditation, and discussions about how faith can help clients cope with their challenges.
7. Advocacy and Support Christian counselors can also play a role in advocating for the needs and rights of people with disabilities. This can include working with clients to navigate the healthcare system, helping clients access resources and services, and advocating for policy changes that promote disability rights.
8. Examples of Empowerment-based Counseling Techniques
   - Goal-setting: Helping clients set achievable goals and develop a plan to reach them
   - Affirmations: Encouraging clients to repeat positive affirmations to themselves
   - Role-playing: Practicing social situations or challenging scenarios to help clients feel more confident and prepared

- Assertiveness training: Teaching clients how to assert their needs and boundaries in social situations

In conclusion, counseling people with disabilities requires a holistic approach that takes into account the physical, social, emotional, and spiritual dimensions of disability. Christian counselors can use a variety of techniques to help clients manage their emotions, build their self-esteem, and connect with their faith. By empowering clients and advocating for their needs, Christian counselors can play an important role in promoting the well-being and dignity of people with disabilities.

5.4 Counseling the LGBTQ+ Community

Counseling the LGBTQ+ Community: Unique Challenges and Techniques for Christian Counselors

As Christian counselors, it is essential to provide a safe and supportive environment for clients who identify as LGBTQ+. These individuals often face unique challenges related to their sexual orientation, gender identity, and religious beliefs. Counselors must be able to address these challenges while also respecting the client's identity and beliefs. This article explores the unique challenges faced by the LGBTQ+ community and offers techniques for counseling this population.

Unique Challenges Faced by the LGBTQ+ Community

The LGBTQ+ community faces several unique challenges that may impact their mental health and wellbeing. Some of these challenges include:

1. Discrimination and Stigma - LGBTQ+ individuals may face discrimination and stigma from their families, friends, co-workers, and even religious communities. This can cause feelings of isolation, shame, and self-doubt.
2. Coming Out - Coming out as LGBTQ+ can be a difficult and emotional process. This can be especially challenging for individuals who come from conservative or religious backgrounds.
3. Mental Health Issues - LGBTQ+ individuals are more likely to experience mental health issues such as anxiety, depression, and substance abuse. These issues may be related to discrimination, stigma, or social isolation.
4. Religious Beliefs - Many LGBTQ+ individuals have religious beliefs that may conflict with their sexual orientation or gender identity. This can cause confusion, guilt, and feelings of alienation.

Techniques for Counseling the LGBTQ+ Community

Counselors who work with the LGBTQ+ community must be aware of these unique challenges and be prepared to offer techniques that promote healing and acceptance. Some techniques that may be used in counseling the LGBTQ+ community include:

1. Affirmative Therapy - Affirmative therapy is a counseling approach that focuses on promoting acceptance and self-esteem for LGBTQ+ clients. The goal of this approach is to help clients embrace their identity and find a sense of belonging.
2. Cognitive-Behavioral Therapy (CBT) - CBT is a counseling technique that helps clients identify and change negative thought patterns. This approach may be helpful for LGBTQ+ clients who struggle with self-doubt or feelings of shame related to their identity.

3. Family Therapy - Family therapy involves working with the client's family to address issues and promote healing. This approach may be helpful for LGBTQ+ clients who are struggling with family acceptance or conflict related to their sexual orientation or gender identity.
4. Mindfulness Techniques - Mindfulness techniques such as deep breathing or visualization can help LGBTQ+ clients manage stress and anxiety related to discrimination, stigma, or social isolation.
5. Spiritual Counseling - For clients who value their religious beliefs, spiritual counseling can help them connect with their faith and find comfort in their spiritual beliefs. This approach may be helpful for LGBTQ+ clients who are struggling with conflicts between their sexual orientation or gender identity and their religious beliefs.
6. Narrative Therapy - Narrative therapy is a counseling technique that helps clients reframe their experiences and gain a new perspective on their identity. This approach may be helpful for LGBTQ+ clients who are struggling with negative self-perceptions or internalized stigma.

Examples of Techniques in Practice

To illustrate how these techniques can be applied in counseling sessions, here are some examples of how Christian counselors may work with LGBTQ+ clients:

- Affirmative therapy may involve exploring the client's values and beliefs related to their sexual orientation or gender identity, and helping them develop a sense of pride and confidence in their identity.
- In CBT, the counselor may help the client identify negative thought patterns related to their sexual

- orientation or gender identity, and work with them to develop more positive and accepting thoughts.
- In family therapy, the counselor may work with the client's family to understand and address any conflicts related to the client's sexual orientation or gender identity. The counselor may help family members learn more about LGBTQ+ issues and offer support and guidance for accepting and affirming their loved one's identity.
- Mindfulness techniques may involve teaching the client relaxation exercises, such as deep breathing or progressive muscle relaxation, to help manage stress and anxiety related to discrimination, stigma, or social isolation.
- Spiritual counseling may involve exploring the client's religious beliefs and values related to their sexual orientation or gender identity. The counselor may help the client find ways to reconcile their faith and their identity and offer support and guidance for spiritual growth and healing.
- Narrative therapy may involve helping the client reframe their experiences related to their sexual orientation or gender identity. The counselor may help the client identify and challenge negative self-perceptions or internalized stigma, and encourage them to create a new narrative that is more accepting and empowering.

In conclusion, counseling the LGBTQ+ community requires sensitivity, awareness, and an understanding of the unique challenges faced by these clients. Christian counselors must be able to provide emotional and spiritual support while also using evidence-based techniques that promote healing and acceptance. By creating a safe and supportive environment, counselors can help their LGBTQ+ clients find the strength and resilience to navigate the challenges of their identity and achieve a sense of wholeness and wellbeing.

Chapter 6: Techniques and Approaches in Christian Counseling

6.1 Cognitive Behavioral Therapy in Christian Counseling

Introduction

Cognitive-behavioral therapy (CBT) is a type of psychotherapy that has been found to be effective in treating a variety of mental health issues. CBT is based on the idea that our thoughts, emotions, and behaviors are interconnected, and that changing one of these can lead to changes in the others. In Christian counseling, CBT can be used to help clients overcome negative thought patterns and beliefs related to their faith and spirituality.

The Intersection of CBT and Christian Counseling

CBT and Christian counseling share many common elements. Both approaches recognize the importance of the mind-body connection and how thoughts and beliefs can impact our emotions and behaviors. Both also emphasize the importance of personal responsibility and encourage individuals to take an active role in their own healing process. However, in Christian counseling, biblical principles and teachings are integrated into the therapy process to provide a spiritual context for healing.

1. Identifying Negative Thoughts and Beliefs: CBT in Christian counseling involves identifying negative thoughts and beliefs related to a client's faith and spirituality. These thoughts may be related to feelings of guilt, shame, or self-doubt. Once identified, a therapist can help the client challenge these thoughts using evidence-based reasoning and biblical principles.
2. Developing Coping Strategies: Coping strategies can help clients manage negative emotions or behaviors related to their faith or spirituality. These strategies may include prayer, meditation, journaling, or other spiritual practices. By developing healthy coping strategies, clients can better manage their emotions and reduce the likelihood of negative behaviors.
3. Setting Goals: Setting goals can help clients focus on positive outcomes and create a roadmap for achieving them. These goals may be related to a client's spiritual growth or other areas of their life. A therapist can help the client create action plans for achieving these goals, using biblical principles to guide the process.
4. Reframing Negative Experiences: CBT in Christian counseling can help clients reframe negative experiences in a more positive light. This may involve exploring biblical teachings related to forgiveness, grace, and redemption. By reframing negative experiences in this way, clients can find meaning and purpose in their suffering.

Benefits of CBT in Christian Counseling

CBT in Christian counseling can provide a number of benefits to clients. By integrating biblical principles and teachings into the therapy process, clients can feel more connected to their faith and spirituality. This can provide a sense of comfort and support during difficult times. Additionally, by using evidence-based techniques, CBT in Christian counseling can help clients develop practical tools for managing their mental health.

Here are some examples of CBT techniques that may be used in Christian counseling:

- Identifying and challenging negative thoughts using evidence-based reasoning and biblical principles
- Developing healthy coping strategies, such as prayer or meditation, to manage negative emotions or behaviors related to faith or spirituality
- Setting goals related to spiritual growth or other areas of life and creating action plans for achieving them
- Reframing negative experiences in a more positive light using biblical teachings related to forgiveness, grace, and redemption

Conclusion

CBT in Christian counseling is an effective approach for helping clients overcome mental health issues related to their faith and spirituality. By integrating biblical principles and teachings into the therapy process, clients can find meaning and purpose in their struggles and develop practical tools for managing their mental health.

6.2 Solution-Focused Therapy in Christian Counseling

Solution-focused therapy is an evidence-based approach that focuses on clients' strengths, resources, and abilities to help them achieve their goals. In Christian counseling, this approach can be tailored to incorporate faith-based principles and practices, helping clients draw on their spiritual beliefs to find meaning, hope, and guidance in their lives.

The primary goal of solution-focused therapy is to help clients identify and build on their existing strengths, resources, and successes. Christian counselors can integrate biblical teachings and practices into this approach, using the client's faith as a foundation for their therapeutic work.

Some key techniques that can be used in solution-focused therapy in Christian counseling include:

1. Identifying Strengths and Resources:

   Christian counselors can help clients identify their strengths and resources, both within and outside of their faith. This may include exploring their spiritual gifts, talents, support systems, and personal qualities that have helped them in the past. By focusing on these strengths, clients can gain a greater sense of self-awareness and confidence, which can help them overcome challenges and achieve their goals.

2. Focusing on Positive Experiences:

   In solution-focused therapy, counselors encourage clients to focus on positive experiences and outcomes. In Christian counseling, this may involve exploring how their faith has brought them comfort, joy, and hope in the past. Counselors can help clients identify positive scriptures, prayer practices, or worship experiences that have been meaningful to them, and use these as a guide for future success.

3. Using Biblical Principles and Teachings:

Christian counselors can incorporate biblical principles and teachings into the therapy process, helping clients develop a positive and hopeful outlook on their lives and circumstances. This may involve exploring relevant scriptures, discussing Christian virtues such as faith, hope, love, and forgiveness, and integrating prayer and spiritual practices into therapy sessions.

4. Developing Action Plans:

Christian counselors can help clients develop action plans for achieving their goals, using a collaborative and supportive approach. This may involve breaking down larger goals into smaller, achievable steps, identifying potential obstacles and ways to overcome them, and celebrating successes along the way.

5. Encouraging Prayer and Spiritual Practices:

In Christian counseling, prayer and spiritual practices can be an essential part of the therapy process. Christian counselors can encourage clients to engage in prayer, meditation, Bible study, and other spiritual practices that align with their faith. These practices can help clients gain perspective, find comfort, and develop a sense of connection to God.

Examples of solution-focused therapy in Christian counseling include:

- Helping a client who is struggling with depression identify positive scriptures that speak to their situation and use them to develop a daily affirmation practice.
- Encouraging a couple who is struggling with communication issues to identify times when they have successfully resolved conflicts in the past and use these as a guide for future conversations.
- Working with a client who is dealing with addiction to identify supportive relationships and faith-based recovery programs that can help them stay sober.
- Helping a client who is feeling overwhelmed by life transitions to develop a vision for their future, using their faith and spiritual beliefs as a foundation for their goals.
- Encouraging a client who is dealing with anxiety to develop a daily gratitude practice, focusing on the positive things in their life and the ways in which God has blessed them.

6.3 Narrative Therapy in Christian Counseling

Overview of Narrative Therapy in Christian Counseling

Narrative therapy is a form of counseling that is based on the idea that people construct stories about their lives, and that these stories can influence how they view themselves, their relationships, and their experiences. In Christian counseling, narrative therapy can be used to help clients explore how their faith and spirituality can be a source of healing and transformation.

1. Identifying Core Values and Beliefs

    One of the first steps in narrative therapy is to help clients identify their core values and beliefs, and how they relate to their experiences and emotions. In Christian counseling, this can involve exploring the client's relationship with God, their understanding of biblical teachings, and their personal beliefs and values.

    By identifying these core beliefs, clients can gain a deeper understanding of how they view themselves and the world around them. This can help them to see how their experiences and emotions may be influenced by their beliefs, and can provide a foundation for exploring new ways of thinking and behaving.

2. Exploring Biblical Principles and Teachings

    Another important aspect of narrative therapy in Christian counseling is to help clients explore different ways of understanding their experiences, using biblical principles and teachings as a guide. This can involve examining stories from the Bible that are relevant to the client's experiences, and discussing how these stories might offer new perspectives on their situation.

    For example, a client who is struggling with feelings of guilt and shame may find comfort in the story of the prodigal son, who is welcomed back into his father's arms despite his mistakes and shortcomings. By exploring these stories, clients can gain new insights into their own lives and can develop a more positive and hopeful narrative.

3. Identifying Strengths and Resources

Another important aspect of narrative therapy is to help clients identify their strengths and resources, and how they can use them to create a positive and meaningful narrative for their lives. In Christian counseling, this can involve exploring how the client's faith and spirituality can be a source of strength and resilience.

For example, a client who is struggling with depression may find that their faith provides them with a sense of purpose and meaning, and can help them to see beyond their current struggles. By identifying these strengths and resources, clients can develop a more positive and hopeful outlook on life.

4. Using Creative Techniques

Finally, narrative therapy in Christian counseling may involve using creative techniques such as journaling, artwork, or storytelling to help clients express their experiences and emotions in a new way. These techniques can be especially helpful for clients who may find it difficult to express themselves through traditional forms of talk therapy.

For example, a client who is struggling with anxiety may find it helpful to create a visual representation of their fears and worries, using art materials such as paint or clay. By externalizing these emotions in a creative way, clients can gain a new perspective on their experiences and can begin to see them in a different light.

- A client who is struggling with addiction may explore their relationship with God and their understanding of biblical teachings on self-control and forgiveness. By reframing their addiction as a spiritual journey, the client can develop a more positive and hopeful narrative for their recovery.
- A client who is dealing with grief and loss may find comfort in exploring biblical stories of loss and mourning, such as the story of Job. By examining these stories and discussing how they relate to their own experiences, the client can gain new insights into their grief and can begin to find hope and healing.
- A client who is experiencing feelings of worthlessness and low self-esteem may be struggling with a number of issues. It is possible that they have been subjected to abuse or neglect, or have experienced significant trauma in their lives. Alternatively, they may be dealing with a mental health condition such as depression or anxiety. In any case, it is important to provide them with a safe, supportive environment in which to explore their feelings and work toward healing and recovery. This might involve therapy, medication, or other forms of treatment, depending on their individual needs and circumstances.

6.4 Mindfulness in Christian Counseling

Mindfulness is a technique that has gained popularity in recent years as a means of managing stress, anxiety, and other negative emotions. It involves being present in the moment and accepting one's experiences without judgment or resistance. In the context of Christian counseling, mindfulness can be used to help clients connect with their faith and spirituality in a deeper and more meaningful way.

Understanding Mindfulness in Christian Counseling

In Christian counseling, mindfulness involves being fully present in the moment and focusing on God's presence in one's life. It is about becoming more aware of one's thoughts, feelings, and bodily sensations, and accepting them without judgment or resistance. Mindfulness can help clients to develop a deeper sense of connection with God and find greater peace and clarity in their lives.

Techniques for Mindfulness in Christian Counseling

There are many different techniques that can be used to promote mindfulness in Christian counseling. Some of these techniques include:

1. Deep breathing exercises

Deep breathing exercises can be a simple but effective way to promote mindfulness in Christian counseling. Examples of deep breathing exercises include the Jesus Prayer and the Examen. The Jesus Prayer involves repeating the phrase "Lord Jesus Christ, have mercy on me" while focusing on one's breath. The Examen is a prayerful reflection on one's day, in which clients focus on their thoughts, feelings, and experiences from the day.

2. Meditation and Visualization Techniques

Meditation and visualization techniques can be a powerful way to promote mindfulness in Christian counseling. These techniques involve using biblical imagery or scripture to focus one's attention and promote a sense of peace and connection with God. Examples of meditation and visualization techniques include meditating on a specific passage of scripture or visualizing oneself in a peaceful, calming scene from the Bible.

3. Mindful Walking or Movement Exercises

Mindful walking or movement exercises can be an effective way to promote mindfulness in Christian counseling. These exercises involve paying close attention to one's movements and bodily sensations while walking or engaging in gentle movement exercises such as yoga or Tai Chi. Clients can also incorporate prayer or scripture reading into these exercises to further deepen their connection with God.

4. Incorporating Mindfulness into Daily Spiritual Practices

Another way to promote mindfulness in Christian counseling is to incorporate it into daily spiritual practices such as prayer or scripture reading. Clients can be encouraged to focus on their breath and bodily sensations while engaging in these practices, and to become more aware of their thoughts and feelings as they do so. By doing this, they can develop a deeper sense of connection with God and find greater peace and clarity in their lives.

There are many benefits of mindfulness in Christian counseling. Some of these benefits include:

- Reduced stress and anxiety
- Improved emotional regulation
- Increased self-awareness
- Greater sense of connection with God
- Enhanced spiritual growth
- Improved overall well-being

Potential Challenges in Mindfulness for Christian Counseling

While mindfulness can be a powerful tool in Christian counseling, there are also potential challenges to be aware of. Some clients may be uncomfortable with mindfulness techniques, or may view them as conflicting with their religious beliefs. It is important for Christian counselors to be respectful of their clients' beliefs and values, and to modify mindfulness techniques as needed to better align with their faith.

Examples of Mindfulness Techniques in Christian Counseling

Here are some specific examples of mindfulness techniques that can be used in Christian counseling:

- Deep breathing exercises, such as the Jesus Prayer or the Examen
- Meditating on a specific passage of scripture or visualizing oneself in a peaceful, calming scene from the Bible

- Mindful walking or movement exercises, such as yoga or Tai Chi
- Practicing gratitude by reflecting on and giving thanks for God's blessings and provisions
- Focusing on the present moment and becoming more aware of one's thoughts, feelings, and bodily sensations
- Using breath prayer or other forms of contemplative prayer to connect with God
- Engaging in journaling or expressive writing as a means of self-reflection and exploration
- Practicing self-compassion and showing oneself the same kindness and compassion as one would show to others

These techniques can be adapted and modified to better align with clients' individual needs and beliefs, and can be used to promote greater mindfulness and connection with God in Christian counseling.

Chapter 7: Christian Counseling in the Church

7.1 The Role of the Church in Christian Counseling

Introduction

The church has the potential to play a significant role in providing counseling services to its members and the wider community. Christian counseling integrates faith and spirituality with evidence-based counseling techniques to help individuals deal with a range of mental health issues.

Christian counseling provides a unique approach to mental health treatment that integrates spirituality and faith with psychological and emotional healing. This approach is particularly important for individuals who want to explore the connection between their spiritual life and their mental health.

The church can provide a safe and supportive environment for individuals seeking Christian counseling services. Many people find comfort in talking to someone who shares their faith and can understand their struggles from a spiritual perspective.

How the Church Can Support Christian Counseling

There are several ways in which the church can support Christian counseling services:

- **Providing Space and Resources**

  The church can provide space and resources for counseling services, such as counseling rooms, support groups, and workshops. Having a dedicated space for counseling services can create a welcoming and safe environment for those seeking help.

- **Offering Training and Education**

  The church can provide training and education for pastoral staff and lay counselors on Christian counseling principles and techniques. This training can help counselors integrate faith and spirituality

into their counseling sessions and provide support
that aligns with the teachings of the church.

- **Collaborating with Mental Health Professionals**

  Collaborating with mental health professionals can
  help the church provide comprehensive care that
  addresses both physical and spiritual needs. This
  collaboration can also help reduce the stigma
  associated with seeking mental health services and
  provide individuals with access to a range of
  treatment options.

- **Promoting Awareness and Understanding**

  The church can promote awareness and
  understanding of mental health issues within the
  church community. By reducing the stigma and
  discrimination associated with mental health,
  individuals may feel more comfortable seeking
  counseling services and getting the help they need.

- **Encouraging the Integration of Faith and
  Spirituality**

  The church can encourage the integration of faith
  and spirituality into counseling sessions. This may
  involve incorporating prayer, scripture, and worship
  services into counseling sessions, or providing
  resources such as devotional materials or spiritual
  exercises.

Benefits of Christian Counseling in the Church

There are many benefits to providing Christian counseling
services within the church:

- **Spiritual Connection**

  Christian counseling provides individuals with the opportunity to explore the connection between their spiritual life and their mental health. By integrating faith and spirituality into counseling sessions, individuals can find greater meaning and purpose in their struggles.

- **Supportive Environment**

  Providing counseling services within the church can create a supportive and safe environment for individuals seeking help. Individuals may feel more comfortable opening up to someone who shares their faith and understands their struggles from a spiritual perspective.

- **Holistic Care**

  Christian counseling provides holistic care that addresses both physical and spiritual needs. By integrating faith and spirituality into counseling sessions, individuals can find healing and wholeness in all aspects of their lives.

Examples of Christian Counseling Services in the Church

There are many different types of Christian counseling services that churches can offer, including:

- Pastoral counseling services: Many churches have pastoral staff who are trained in Christian counseling and provide counseling services to their congregation.

- Support groups: Churches can offer support groups for individuals dealing with specific issues, such as addiction recovery or grief and loss.
- Workshops and seminars: Churches can offer workshops and seminars on topics related to mental health and spirituality, such as stress management or forgiveness.
- Referral services: Churches can provide referral services for individuals seeking professional mental health services, such as psychologists or therapists.

7.2 Pastoral Counseling

What is Pastoral Counseling?

Pastoral counseling is a form of therapy that is grounded in the Christian faith and provided by trained pastors or other pastoral staff members within a church setting. The goal of pastoral counseling is to provide individuals with holistic care that addresses not only their psychological and emotional needs but also their spiritual well-being.

Benefits of Pastoral Counseling

Pastoral counseling can be a valuable form of therapy for individuals who are struggling with issues related to their faith or spirituality. It can provide a safe and supportive environment where individuals can explore their beliefs and values while also receiving mental health care. Some of the benefits of pastoral counseling include:

- Addressing both psychological and spiritual needs
- Providing a faith-based approach to mental health care
- Promoting spiritual growth and development
- Offering guidance and support during difficult times

- Encouraging a sense of community and connection with others

Techniques Used in Pastoral Counseling

Pastoral counselors use a range of techniques to help individuals address their spiritual and emotional needs. These techniques may include:

- Biblical teachings and principles: Pastoral counselors may use scripture and other biblical teachings to guide the therapy process.
- Prayer and meditation: Pastoral counseling may incorporate prayer and meditation to help individuals connect with their spiritual selves and seek guidance from a higher power.
- Active listening and empathy: Pastoral counselors create a supportive environment where individuals can feel heard and understood.
- Reframing and cognitive restructuring: Pastoral counselors may use techniques from cognitive-behavioral therapy to help individuals identify and challenge negative thought patterns.
- Self-reflection and introspection: Pastoral counseling may encourage individuals to reflect on their own beliefs and values and explore how they can integrate these into their daily lives.

Examples of Issues Addressed through Pastoral Counseling

Pastoral counseling can address a wide range of issues, including:

- Anxiety and depression
- Grief and loss
- Relationship issues

- Spiritual crises or questioning
- Stress management
- Addiction and substance abuse
- Trauma and abuse
- Marital problems
- Parenting difficulties

Conclusion

Pastoral counseling is a form of therapy that provides individuals with a holistic approach to mental health care. By addressing both psychological and spiritual needs, pastoral counseling can help individuals find meaning, purpose, and healing in their lives. If you're struggling with issues related to your faith or spirituality, or if you're seeking a more holistic approach to mental health care, pastoral counseling may be a helpful option to consider.

7.3 Lay Counseling Programs

What are Lay Counseling Programs?

Lay counseling programs are community-based initiatives that provide basic counseling services to individuals in need, often in partnership with local churches or other faith-based organizations. Lay counselors are individuals who have received training in basic counseling techniques and are able to provide support and guidance to those in need, particularly those who may not have access to licensed mental health professionals.

Benefits of Lay Counseling Programs

Lay counseling programs can provide a range of benefits to individuals who may be struggling with mental health issues or other life challenges. Some of the benefits of lay counseling programs include:

- Increased access to counseling services: Lay counseling programs can provide counseling services to individuals who may not have access to licensed mental health professionals or who may not be able to afford professional counseling services.
- Greater sense of community: Lay counseling programs often operate in partnership with local churches or other faith-based organizations, providing individuals with a sense of community and connection.
- Holistic approach to mental health care: Lay counseling programs may incorporate faith-based approaches to counseling, which can provide a more holistic approach to mental health care.
- Support and guidance: Lay counselors are often able to provide ongoing support and guidance to individuals in need, helping them to navigate life's challenges and develop coping skills.

Some of the key principles of lay counseling programs include:

- Providing basic counseling services: Lay counseling programs focus on providing basic counseling services that are grounded in Christian principles and values.
- Offering support and guidance: Lay counselors provide support and guidance to individuals in need, helping them to navigate life's challenges and develop coping skills.
- Referring clients to licensed mental health professionals: Lay counselors are not licensed mental health professionals and may not be equipped to address complex mental health issues. As such, they

may refer clients to licensed mental health professionals for more comprehensive care.
- Providing ongoing training and support: Lay counselors receive ongoing training and support to ensure that they are providing effective and ethical services.

Techniques Used in Lay Counseling

Lay counselors may use a range of techniques to help individuals in need. These may include:

- Active listening and empathy: Lay counselors create a supportive environment where individuals can feel heard and understood.
- Reframing and cognitive restructuring: Lay counselors may use techniques from cognitive-behavioral therapy to help individuals identify and challenge negative thought patterns.
- Prayer and meditation: Lay counseling may incorporate prayer and meditation to help individuals connect with their spiritual selves and seek guidance from a higher power.
- Self-reflection and introspection: Lay counseling may encourage individuals to reflect on their own beliefs and values and explore how they can integrate these into their daily lives.

Examples of Issues Addressed through Lay Counseling

Lay counseling programs can address a wide range of issues, including:

- Stress and anxiety
- Depression
- Relationship issues
- Parenting difficulties

- Grief and loss
- Addiction and substance abuse
- Anger management
- Self-esteem issues
- Trauma and abuse

Conclusion

Lay counseling programs can be a valuable way for communities to provide support and guidance to individuals in need, particularly those who may not have access to licensed mental health professionals. By providing basic counseling services that are grounded in Christian principles and values, lay counseling programs can help individuals to navigate life's challenges and develop coping skills that can help them to lead happier, healthier lives.

What are Lay Counseling Programs?

Lay counseling programs are community-based initiatives that provide basic counseling services to individuals in need, often in partnership with local churches or other faith-based organizations. Lay counselors are individuals who have received training in basic counseling techniques and are able to provide support and guidance to those in need, particularly those who may not have access to licensed mental health professionals.

Benefits of Lay Counseling Programs

Lay counseling programs can provide a range of benefits to individuals who may be struggling with mental health issues or other life challenges. Some of the benefits of lay counseling programs include:

- Increased access to counseling services: Lay counseling programs can provide counseling services to individuals who may not have access to licensed mental health professionals or who may not be able to afford professional counseling services.
- Greater sense of community: Lay counseling programs often operate in partnership with local churches or other faith-based organizations, providing individuals with a sense of community and connection.
- Holistic approach to mental health care: Lay counseling programs may incorporate faith-based approaches to counseling, which can provide a more holistic approach to mental health care.
- Support and guidance: Lay counselors are often able to provide ongoing support and guidance to individuals in need, helping them to navigate life's challenges and develop coping skills.

Key Principles of Lay Counseling Programs

Some of the key principles of lay counseling programs include:

- Providing basic counseling services: Lay counseling programs focus on providing basic counseling services that are grounded in Christian principles and values.
- Offering support and guidance: Lay counselors provide support and guidance to individuals in need, helping them to navigate life's challenges and develop coping skills.
- Referring clients to licensed mental health professionals: Lay counselors are not licensed mental health professionals and may not be equipped to address complex mental health issues. As such, they may refer clients to licensed mental health professionals for more comprehensive care.

- Providing ongoing training and support: Lay counselors receive ongoing training and support to ensure that they are providing effective and ethical services.

Techniques Used in Lay Counseling

Lay counselors may use a range of techniques to help individuals in need. These may include:

- Active listening and empathy: Lay counselors create a supportive environment where individuals can feel heard and understood.
- Reframing and cognitive restructuring: Lay counselors may use techniques from cognitive-behavioral therapy to help individuals identify and challenge negative thought patterns.
- Prayer and meditation: Lay counseling may incorporate prayer and meditation to help individuals connect with their spiritual selves and seek guidance from a higher power.
- Self-reflection and introspection: Lay counseling may encourage individuals to reflect on their own beliefs and values and explore how they can integrate these into their daily lives.

Examples of Issues Addressed through Lay Counseling

Lay counseling programs can address a wide range of issues, including:

- Stress and anxiety
- Depression
- Relationship issues
- Parenting difficulties
- Grief and loss
- Addiction and substance abuse

- Anger management
- Self-esteem issues
- Trauma and abuse

Lay counseling programs can be a valuable way for communities to provide support and guidance to individuals in need, particularly those who may not have access to licensed mental health professionals. By providing basic counseling services that are grounded in Christian principles and values, lay counseling programs can help individuals to navigate life's challenges and develop coping skills that can help them to lead happier, healthier lives.

7.4 Church-Based Support Groups

Church-based support groups are a valuable resource for individuals who are seeking support and healing in a safe and nurturing environment. These groups provide a space for individuals to come together and share their experiences, struggles, and hopes in a supportive community. By connecting with others who have similar experiences, participants can feel less alone and more understood.

These groups can be led by trained facilitators who have the skills and knowledge to guide the group through the healing process. They can also be led by peer support leaders who have personal experience with the challenges that the group members are facing. Either way, the group leader is responsible for creating a safe and supportive environment that fosters healing and growth.

Many church-based support groups are grounded in biblical teachings and principles. This means that participants can draw on the wisdom and guidance of the Bible to help them navigate their struggles and find hope in difficult times. However, these groups are open to people of all faiths and backgrounds, and participants are not required to have any particular religious affiliation.

Overall, church-based support groups are a valuable resource for anyone who is looking to connect with others and find support and healing in a safe and nurturing environment. Whether you are struggling with addiction, grief, mental health issues, or any other challenge, these groups can provide the support and encouragement you need to move forward on your journey toward healing and wholeness.

Benefits of Church-Based Support Groups

Church-based support groups offer many benefits to individuals who are struggling with various issues. Some of these benefits include:

- A safe and supportive environment: Church-based support groups provide a safe and supportive environment where individuals can share their experiences and struggles with others who understand what they are going through.
- Guidance and support from others: Group members can offer guidance, support, and encouragement to one another, providing a sense of community and belonging.
- Use of biblical teachings and principles: Many church-based support groups incorporate biblical teachings and principles into their programs, which can provide a sense of spiritual grounding and hope.

- Active participation in healing process: Church-based support groups encourage individuals to take an active role in their own healing process, which can lead to greater feelings of empowerment and control.

Church-based support groups can be organized around various themes or issues, such as:

- Addiction and recovery
- Mental health and wellness
- Grief and loss
- Relationship and family issues
- Financial stewardship
- Spiritual growth and development

Church-based support groups can vary in structure and format depending on the needs of the group members and the goals of the program. Some common features of support groups include:

- Regular meetings: Groups typically meet on a regular basis, such as weekly or biweekly.
- Facilitator or peer support leader: The group is typically led by a facilitator or peer support leader who is trained to provide guidance and support to group members.
- Confidentiality: Group members are often asked to maintain confidentiality to create a safe and trusting environment.
- Sharing and discussion: Group members are encouraged to share their experiences and struggles and engage in discussion with other members.

- Education and resources: Many groups offer educational materials and resources to help members better understand their issues and develop coping skills.

- Celebrate Recovery: A Christ-centered 12-step program that provides support and healing to individuals struggling with addiction and other life issues.
- GriefShare: A support group for individuals who are grieving the loss of a loved one, which provides comfort, encouragement, and practical advice for dealing with grief.
- DivorceCare: A support group for individuals who are going through or have gone through a divorce, which offers guidance and support for healing and growth.
- Mental Health Grace Alliance: A program that offers a variety of support groups and resources to individuals and families affected by mental health issues.
- Financial Peace University: A program that provides support and guidance to individuals seeking to improve their financial health and stewardship.

In conclusion, church-based support groups can be a valuable resource for individuals seeking support and healing in a safe and nurturing environment. By offering a variety of groups that incorporate biblical teachings and principles, the church can help individuals address a wide range of issues and find hope and healing in their lives.

Chapter 8: Integrating Faith and Psychology

Christian counseling is a very special approach to mental health treatment that incorporates faith and spirituality into evidence-based counseling techniques. This unique approach provides people with the opportunity to explore the relationship between faith and psychology, while addressing their mental health needs.

The relationship between faith and psychology can be complex and challenging, as each field has its own unique perspectives and assumptions. However, Christian counseling offers a way to bridge the gap between these fields and to provide a holistic approach to mental health treatment.

Integrating faith and psychology in Christian counseling can also be a challenging task. It requires not only a deep understanding of both fields, but also an ability to navigate the potential conflicts that can arise. However, with the right training and guidance, Christian counselors can provide effective treatment that is grounded in both faith and science.

Best practices for integrating faith and psychology in Christian counseling include building a strong therapeutic relationship, incorporating prayer and scripture into therapy, and utilizing evidence-based techniques that are consistent with Christian values. By following these best practices, Christian counselors can provide effective treatment that addresses the unique needs of their clients.

8.1 Christian Psychology and Christian Counseling

Christian psychology and Christian counseling are two fields that aim to incorporate Christian beliefs and principles into psychological theory and practice. However, despite their similarities, there are some differences between the two. Christian psychology is more focused on the study of human behavior and how it relates to Christian beliefs, while Christian counseling places a greater emphasis on the practical application of Christian principles in counseling sessions.

Both fields share a common goal of providing a more holistic approach to mental health care, which involves considering all aspects of a person's life, including their faith and spirituality. This approach recognizes that mental health is not just about the absence of mental illness, but rather the presence of positive well-being in all areas of life. Incorporating faith and spirituality into the therapy process can help individuals find meaning and purpose in life, develop a sense of hope and resilience, and experience greater levels of satisfaction and fulfillment.

In addition, Christian psychology and Christian counseling can also help individuals develop a better understanding of their relationship with God and how it impacts their emotional and mental health. This can lead to a deeper sense of self-awareness and a greater sense of connection with others and with God.

Overall, Christian psychology and Christian counseling provide a unique perspective on mental health care that can benefit individuals from all walks of life, regardless of their religious beliefs. By integrating faith and spirituality into the therapy process, these fields offer a more comprehensive approach to mental health care that recognizes the importance of addressing all aspects of a person's life in order to promote greater well-being and overall health.

Christian psychology is grounded in the belief that human beings are created in the image of God, and that this image is reflected in their physical, emotional, intellectual, and spiritual dimensions. This belief has important implications for how Christian psychologists view human nature and the purpose of psychology.

Some of the key theoretical foundations of Christian psychology include:

- A belief in the dignity and worth of every human being
- A focus on the spiritual dimensions of human life
- A belief in the possibility of transformation and growth through faith

Integration of Faith and Psychology

Christian psychology seeks to integrate Christian beliefs and principles with psychological theory and practice. This involves a dialogue between faith and psychology, in which insights from both disciplines are used to understand human nature and promote healing and wholeness.

Some of the ways in which Christian psychologists integrate faith and psychology include:

- Using biblical teachings and principles to guide the therapy process
- Incorporating prayer and spiritual practices into therapy sessions
- Viewing psychological issues through a spiritual lens
- Encouraging clients to draw on their faith for strength and guidance

Christian counseling is a form of therapy that is grounded in Christian principles and values. It seeks to integrate faith and spirituality with evidence-based counseling techniques to help individuals deal with a range of mental health issues.

Some of the key principles of Christian counseling include:

- A focus on the whole person, including their spiritual, emotional, and physical dimensions
- A belief in the power of faith to promote healing and transformation
- A commitment to providing care and support in the context of a Christian community
- A recognition of the importance of professional ethics and standards in counseling practice

Examples of Christian Psychology and Christian Counseling

Here are some examples of Christian psychology and Christian counseling in practice:

- A Christian psychologist might use insights from psychology and theology to help a client overcome feelings of guilt and shame related to past mistakes.
- A Christian counselor might use evidence-based techniques such as cognitive-behavioral therapy to help a client manage symptoms of anxiety, while also incorporating prayer and spiritual practices into therapy sessions.
- A Christian support group might use biblical teachings and principles to provide support and encouragement to individuals struggling with addiction or grief.

In conclusion, Christian psychology and Christian counseling offer a unique approach to mental health care that integrates faith and spirituality with evidence-based psychological theory and practice. They provide a holistic approach to healing and transformation that can be especially meaningful to individuals who share a Christian worldview.

8.2 Challenges in Integrating Faith and Psychology

Integrating faith and psychology can be challenging for a number of reasons. Some of the key challenges include:

- Differing Worldviews

  Psychologists and counselors may have different worldviews and beliefs that can make it difficult to integrate faith and psychology in a way that is meaningful and effective. Christian psychologists and counselors may approach mental health issues from a perspective that emphasizes the importance of faith, while secular psychologists and counselors may view mental health issues primarily as biological or psychological in nature. This can create tension and conflict in the therapy process and may make it difficult to find common ground between the two perspectives.

- Stigma and Discrimination

  Mental health issues are often stigmatized and discriminated against, which can make it difficult for individuals to seek counseling services that integrate faith and spirituality. Some individuals may feel ashamed or embarrassed to seek help for mental health issues and may be hesitant to seek help from a Christian counselor or psychologist due to fears of being judged or rejected by their community.

- Lack of Training and Education

Psychologists and counselors may not have the necessary training and education to effectively integrate faith and psychology in their work. Christian counselors and psychologists may require additional training in theology and biblical studies to effectively incorporate faith into their practice. Likewise, secular counselors and psychologists may require additional training in religious and spiritual practices to understand and respect the role of faith in their clients' lives.

- Ethical Concerns

Integrating faith and psychology can raise ethical concerns, such as respecting clients' beliefs and values and avoiding imposing one's own beliefs on clients. Christian counselors and psychologists must be careful not to impose their own beliefs on clients and should seek to understand and respect their clients' beliefs and values. Likewise, secular counselors and psychologists should be respectful of their clients' faith and should not attempt to change or discredit their beliefs.

- Lack of Research

There is a lack of empirical research on the effectiveness of integrating faith and psychology in counseling and therapy. While there is anecdotal evidence to suggest that Christian counseling and psychology can be effective in promoting mental health and well-being, more research is needed to determine the efficacy of these approaches.

Despite the challenges, there are many potential benefits to integrating faith and psychology in counseling and therapy. Some of the key benefits include:

- Holistic Approach

  Integrating faith and psychology can provide a more holistic approach to mental health care, addressing not only the biological and psychological aspects of mental health, but also the spiritual and emotional aspects.

- Meaning and Purpose

  For individuals who place a high value on faith and spirituality, integrating these aspects into the therapy process can provide a sense of meaning and purpose, and can help individuals find hope and healing in difficult times.

- Sense of Community

  Integrating faith and psychology can provide a sense of community and support for individuals who may feel isolated or disconnected from their community. Christian counseling and psychology can provide a supportive and compassionate environment where individuals can share their experiences and receive support and encouragement from others.

- Improved Outcomes

  While more research is needed, there is anecdotal evidence to suggest that integrating faith and psychology in counseling and therapy can lead to improved outcomes for clients, including reduced symptoms of anxiety and depression, improved relationships, and a greater sense of well-being.

Examples of Integrating Faith and Psychology

There are many different approaches to integrating faith and psychology in counseling and therapy. Some examples include:

- Christian counseling and psychology: These approaches integrate faith and spirituality with evidence-based counseling techniques to help individuals deal with a range of mental health issues.
- Spiritual direction: This approach focuses on helping individuals discern and deepen their relationship with God, and can be useful for individuals who are seeking guidance in their spiritual lives.

Despite these challenges, integrating faith and psychology can be a valuable and effective approach to mental health care. It can provide a more holistic and personalized approach to therapy that addresses both the spiritual and emotional needs of clients.

To address these challenges, efforts have been made to increase awareness and education around the integration of faith and psychology. Training programs and resources are available to help psychologists and counselors develop the skills and knowledge necessary to effectively integrate faith and spirituality into their work.

Additionally, some organizations and institutions have developed guidelines and ethical standards for integrating faith and psychology. These standards aim to promote ethical and effective integration of faith and psychology in therapy, while also respecting the beliefs and values of clients.

Overall, while there are challenges to integrating faith and psychology, it can be a valuable approach to mental health care that provides a more holistic and personalized form of therapy. With increased awareness, education, and ethical standards, the integration of faith and psychology can continue to be an effective and meaningful approach to mental health care.

8.3 Best Practices for Integrating Faith and Psychology

Integrating Faith and Psychology in Different Settings

The integration of faith and psychology can take place in a variety of settings, including:

- Private practice: Psychologists and counselors in private practice may integrate faith and psychology in their work by incorporating prayer, scripture, and other spiritual practices into counseling sessions.
- Church-based counseling services: Churches may offer counseling services that integrate faith and psychology, such as lay counseling programs or support groups.

- Christian universities and colleges: Many Christian universities and colleges offer graduate programs in Christian counseling and psychology, providing opportunities for students to integrate their faith and psychology education.
- Community mental health centers: Community mental health centers may offer Christian counseling services or have counselors who are trained in Christian counseling.

Examples of Christian Counseling Techniques

There are several techniques and approaches used in Christian counseling that can help individuals address mental health issues while incorporating faith and spirituality. Some examples include:

- Biblical counseling: This approach uses the Bible as a source of guidance and support for individuals dealing with mental health issues.
- Prayer therapy: This technique involves using prayer as a form of therapy to promote healing and wholeness.
- Forgiveness therapy: Forgiveness therapy helps individuals let go of grudges and negative feelings, which can lead to improved mental health and wellbeing.
- Spiritual direction: This approach involves helping individuals connect with their faith and spirituality in a deeper way, which can lead to improved mental and emotional health.

Ethics and Christian Counseling

Integrating faith and psychology in counseling raises ethical concerns that must be addressed to provide ethical and effective care. Some key ethical considerations in Christian counseling include:

- Informed consent: Clients must be fully informed about the nature and purpose of Christian counseling, including any religious beliefs or practices that will be incorporated into the counseling process.
- Boundaries: Psychologists and counselors must maintain appropriate boundaries with their clients and avoid imposing their own beliefs or values on them.
- Confidentiality: Christian counselors must adhere to the same ethical guidelines regarding confidentiality as non-faith-based counselors.
- Referral: If a client's beliefs or values conflict with the Christian counselor's beliefs or values, the counselor should make an appropriate referral to another counselor who can provide effective and appropriate care.

Integrating faith and psychology in counseling can provide several benefits to individuals seeking mental health care. Some of the benefits include:

- A more holistic approach to care: By integrating faith and spirituality into counseling, individuals can address not only their mental health needs but also their spiritual needs.
- Improved coping skills: Faith and spirituality can provide individuals with coping skills and resources that can help them deal with mental health issues.
- Enhanced sense of meaning and purpose: Connecting with one's faith and spirituality can provide individuals with a sense of meaning and purpose that can promote mental health and well-being.

- Greater sense of support: Integrating faith and spirituality into counseling can provide individuals with a sense of support and community that can be invaluable in the healing process.

Here are some examples of Christian counseling services that are available to individuals seeking mental health care:

- Focus on the Family Counseling Services: Focus on the Family offers Christian counseling services for individuals and families dealing with a range of mental health issues.
- Christian Counseling Associates: This organization provides Christian counseling services in various locations throughout the United States.
- American Association of Christian Counselors: The AACC offers resources and referrals for individuals seeking Christian counseling services.
- New Life Ministries: New Life Ministries offers Christian counseling services and resources for individuals and families dealing with mental health issues.

Chapter 9: Ethics in Christian Counseling

9.1 Code of Ethics for Christian Counselors

Christian counselors are held to high ethical standards that are grounded in Christian principles and values. These standards are designed to ensure that all clients receive effective and ethical care that is consistent with Christian beliefs and values. Christian counselors are expected to provide an environment that is conducive to spiritual growth and emotional healing. They should be knowledgeable about Christian teachings and apply them appropriately in their counseling practice. Additionally, Christian counselors must be sensitive to the diverse needs of their clients and respect their cultural and religious backgrounds. They must also maintain confidentiality and ensure that their clients' privacy is protected. Ultimately, Christian counselors have a responsibility to care for the whole person, addressing their physical, emotional, and spiritual needs, and to help them achieve their goals in life by applying Christian values and principles to their practice.

- Respecting the Dignity and Worth of Every Individual

  Christian counselors are called to respect the dignity and worth of every individual, as all people are created in the image of God. This means that Christian counselors should avoid discriminating against clients based on their race, ethnicity, gender, sexual orientation, or any other characteristic. Christian counselors should also strive to create a safe and inclusive environment where all clients feel respected and valued.

- Maintaining Confidentiality and Privacy

  Confidentiality and privacy are crucial components of the counseling relationship. Christian counselors are called to maintain the confidentiality of their clients' information, unless disclosure is required by law or necessary to prevent harm to the client or others. Christian counselors should also ensure that clients' privacy is protected and that their information is stored securely.

- Providing Competent and Ethical Services

Christian counselors are expected to provide competent and ethical services that are consistent with Christian beliefs and values. This may involve integrating faith and spirituality into counseling sessions, but it also requires a deep understanding of evidence-based counseling techniques and best practices. Christian counselors should continually seek to improve their knowledge and skills through professional development and ongoing education.

- Avoiding Harm to Clients

Christian counselors have a duty to avoid causing harm to their clients. This means that they should strive to provide counseling services that are beneficial to their clients and avoid engaging in any behavior that could be detrimental to their clients' well-being.

- Respecting Cultural and Individual Diversity

Christian counselors should respect the cultural and individual diversity of their clients. This means that they should be aware of their own biases and strive to provide culturally sensitive and appropriate care to all clients, regardless of their background or beliefs.

- Providing Informed Consent

Christian counselors are required to obtain informed consent from their clients before providing any counseling services. This means that clients should be fully informed about the nature of the counseling services, the potential benefits and risks, and their rights as clients. Christian counselors should also ensure that clients have the opportunity to ask questions and make informed decisions about their care.

- Maintaining Appropriate Boundaries

Christian counselors should maintain appropriate boundaries with their clients. This means avoiding any behavior that could be perceived as exploitative, manipulative, or abusive. Christian counselors should also avoid engaging in any dual relationships with their clients, such as providing counseling services to a family member or friend.

Examples of Ethical Dilemmas for Christian Counselors

Christian counselors may face a variety of ethical dilemmas in their work, such as:

- A client who wants to discuss their same-sex attraction, but the counselor's religious beliefs condemn homosexuality
- A client who wants to terminate counseling, but the counselor believes that they are not yet ready to do so
- A client who wants to discuss their religious beliefs, but the counselor feels uncomfortable talking about religion
- A client who wants to end their life, but the counselor's religious beliefs forbid suicide

In each of these situations, Christian counselors must balance their personal beliefs and values with their ethical obligations to provide competent and ethical care to their clients. By following the principles outlined in the Code of Ethics for Christian Counselors, Christian counselors can navigate these ethical dilemmas in a way that is consistent with Christian beliefs and values while still providing effective and ethical care to their clients.

9.2 Confidentiality in Christian Counseling

Confidentiality is a foundational aspect of Christian counseling, as it is crucial for clients to feel safe and secure when sharing their thoughts, feelings, and experiences with their counselor. In addition to the ethical standards of counseling, Christian counselors are also guided by biblical principles of trust, honesty, and respect for privacy. As such, confidentiality is taken seriously and should be carefully maintained throughout the counseling process.

There are several key aspects of confidentiality that Christian counselors should consider:

1. Providing clear and comprehensive information about the limits of confidentiality: It is essential for Christian counselors to provide clients with clear and detailed information about what information will be kept confidential and what circumstances may require the counselor to breach confidentiality. Counselors should provide this information in a way that is easy to understand and should encourage clients to ask questions and seek clarification.
2. Obtaining written consent from clients before disclosing any information: Before disclosing any confidential information, Christian counselors should obtain written consent from their clients. This consent should be

specific to the information that will be disclosed and should be obtained in a manner that respects the client's autonomy and right to privacy.

3. Ensuring that all records and documentation are kept confidential and secure: Christian counselors must ensure that all records and documentation related to their clients are kept confidential and secure. This includes paper records, electronic records, and any other documentation that contains sensitive information about clients.

4. Disclosing confidential information only when legally required or when there is a risk of harm to the client or others: Christian counselors may be required to disclose confidential information in certain circumstances, such as when there is a legal obligation to do so or when there is a risk of harm to the client or others. In these situations, counselors should take appropriate steps to protect confidentiality while also complying with legal requirements.

5. Understanding potential challenges to confidentiality: Christian counselors should be aware of potential challenges to confidentiality, such as mandated reporting laws, court orders, or requests for information from third parties. In these situations, counselors should take appropriate steps to protect confidentiality while also complying with legal requirements.

6. Maintaining confidentiality outside of the counseling session: Christian counselors should also be mindful of maintaining confidentiality outside of the counseling session. This includes being mindful of conversations that may take place outside of the counseling session and taking steps to ensure that confidential information is not inadvertently disclosed.

Examples of situations where confidentiality may need to be breached include:

- If the client is a minor and is being abused or neglected by a caregiver
- If the client expresses a desire to harm themselves or others
- If the client discloses information about ongoing criminal activity
- If the client discloses information about ongoing child abuse or neglect

In conclusion, confidentiality is a crucial aspect of Christian counseling, and Christian counselors must take steps to maintain confidentiality throughout the counseling process. By providing clear and comprehensive information about confidentiality, obtaining written consent, and ensuring that all records and documentation are kept confidential and secure, Christian counselors can create a safe and secure environment for their clients to receive counseling services.

9.3 Dual Relationships in Christian Counseling

Dual relationships occur when a counselor has multiple roles or relationships with a client, which can create conflicts of interest and potentially compromise the therapeutic relationship. These relationships may include serving as both a counselor and a friend, providing counseling to a family member or close friend, or engaging in a business or financial relationship with a client.

While dual relationships are not inherently unethical, they can present significant ethical challenges in Christian counseling. Christian counselors must be aware of the potential risks and take appropriate steps to avoid or manage them, while also remaining committed to providing effective and ethical care to their clients.

Some important considerations for Christian counselors in managing dual relationships include:

Establishing Boundaries and Expectations for the Counseling Relationship

Establishing clear boundaries and expectations for the counseling relationship can help minimize the risks associated with dual relationships. Counselors should be transparent with their clients about the boundaries of their relationship and avoid engaging in any activities or behaviors that could compromise the therapeutic relationship. They should also strive to maintain a professional demeanor and avoid engaging in any activities that may be seen as favoritism or partiality.

Obtaining Informed Consent

Obtaining informed consent is an essential part of managing dual relationships in Christian counseling. Before engaging in any potential dual relationships, counselors should obtain written consent from their clients. This consent should be specific to the relationship and should clearly outline the potential risks and benefits of engaging in the dual relationship. Counselors should also encourage their clients to ask questions and seek clarification before giving their consent.

One of the most effective ways to manage dual relationships is to avoid them whenever possible. While it may not always be feasible to avoid all dual relationships, Christian counselors should be mindful of the potential risks and consider alternative options when possible. For example, if a counselor is asked to provide counseling to a close friend or family member, they may consider referring the individual to another counselor to avoid a potential conflict of interest.

Consulting with Colleagues or Supervisors

Consulting with colleagues or supervisors can be an effective way to manage dual relationships and ensure ethical decision-making. When faced with a potential dual relationship, Christian counselors should consult with their colleagues or supervisors to discuss the situation and explore alternative options. This can help counselors make informed decisions and avoid potential ethical dilemmas.

Examples of dual relationships that Christian counselors may encounter include:

- Providing counseling to a close family member or friend
- Serving as both a counselor and a spiritual advisor to a client
- Providing counseling to a member of a congregation or church where the counselor is also a member or leader
- Engaging in a business or financial relationship with a client
- Serving as both a counselor and an employer or supervisor to a client

In conclusion, managing dual relationships is a complex and ongoing process that requires Christian counselors to be mindful of the potential risks and challenges. By establishing clear boundaries and expectations for the counseling relationship, obtaining informed consent, avoiding dual relationships whenever possible, and consulting with colleagues or supervisors, Christian counselors can help ensure ethical decision-making and provide effective and ethical care to their clients.

Chapter 10: Legal Issues in Christian Counseling

10.1 Legal Requirements for Christian Counselors

Christian counselors are subject to a variety of legal requirements that govern their practice. These requirements may include obtaining a license to practice, adhering to professional standards and ethical guidelines, and complying with state and federal laws related to mental health care. Christian counselors must be aware of these legal requirements and ensure that they are in compliance to avoid potential legal liability and disciplinary action.

Licensure and Certification

In most states, Christian counselors are required to obtain a license or certification to practice. This is an important step in ensuring that counselors meet certain standards of education and training, and are equipped to provide high-quality care to their clients. To obtain a license or certification, Christian counselors typically must complete a master's or doctoral degree in counseling or a related field. During this time, they will gain a deep understanding of the theories and techniques that underpin counseling, as well as the ethical guidelines that govern the profession.

Once they have completed their degree, Christian counselors must pass a state licensing exam. This exam is designed to test their knowledge and skills, and ensure that they are able to provide effective counseling services to their clients. In addition to passing the exam, counselors must also complete a certain number of supervised clinical hours. This allows them to gain hands-on experience working with clients, under the guidance of an experienced counselor.

It is also important for Christian counselors to adhere to continuing education requirements in order to maintain their licensure or certification. This ensures that they stay up-to-date with the latest research and best practices in the field of counseling, and are able to provide their clients with the highest level of care possible. By staying current with continuing education, Christian counselors can also expand their knowledge and skills, and specialize in areas such as trauma counseling or family therapy.

Ethical and Professional Standards

Christian counselors are subject to ethical and professional standards that are established by professional organizations such as the American Counseling Association (ACA) and the American Association of Christian Counselors (AACC). These organizations provide ongoing training, continuing education, and resources to ensure that counselors are up-to-date on the latest research and best practices in the field. In addition to these standards, Christian counselors are also guided by their own personal values and beliefs, which can influence their approach to counseling. For example, some Christian counselors may use prayer or scripture as a part of their counseling sessions, while others may not. It is important for clients to understand their counselor's approach and values so that they can make an informed decision about whether the counselor is a good fit for their needs. Furthermore, adherence to these standards is not only important for ethical and legal reasons, but it is also crucial for building trust and rapport with clients. Clients are more likely to feel comfortable and open up to a counselor who they trust and believe has their best interests in mind. By following these standards, Christian counselors can demonstrate their commitment to their clients' well-being and establish a foundation of trust that can lead to positive outcomes in counseling. However, failure to adhere to these standards can result in disciplinary action, which can damage a counselor's reputation and potentially harm their clients. Therefore, it is essential for Christian counselors to take these standards seriously and to continuously strive to improve their practice through ongoing training and self-reflection.

State and Federal Laws

Christian counselors play a vital role in the mental health care system, providing support and guidance to those in need. It is important to recognize, however, that with great responsibility comes great accountability. Christian counselors must abide by state and federal laws related to mental health care, which can encompass a wide range of regulations. These may include requirements related to the confidentiality of client information, reporting obligations for child abuse or neglect, and mandatory protocols for communicating information about certain communicable diseases. Thus, Christian counselors must maintain a comprehensive understanding of these laws and the implications of non-compliance, in order to ensure that they are providing the highest standard of care while avoiding potential legal liability.

10.2 Liability in Christian Counseling

Christian counselors may be subject to legal liability if they engage in behavior that causes harm to their clients. This could include negligent or intentional behavior that results in physical, emotional, or financial harm to the client. Liability can arise from a variety of situations, including failure to obtain informed consent, breach of confidentiality, or failure to provide competent and ethical care. The consequences of legal liability can be severe, including financial damages, loss of reputation, and even legal sanctions.

To minimize their liability risk, it is important for Christian counselors to maintain clear and accurate records of their interactions with clients, including documentation of informed consent and any disclosures made to the client. It is also important for counselors to stay up-to-date with the latest ethical guidelines and legal requirements in their field, and to regularly assess and monitor their own competence and effectiveness as a counselor.

In addition to these steps, Christian counselors can also take proactive measures to ensure that they are providing effective and ethical care to their clients. This might include ongoing training and education, consultation with colleagues or supervisors, and regular self-reflection and evaluation of their counseling practices. By taking these steps, Christian counselors can help to minimize their liability risk and provide the best possible care to their clients.

Informed Consent

Obtaining informed consent is a critical aspect of minimizing liability risk in Christian counseling. It is essential for Christian counselors to provide clients with detailed information about the nature of counseling services, including the techniques and methods used, the potential risks and benefits, and their rights as clients. Some of the risks that may arise during counseling include the possibility that the client may experience emotional distress, that difficult memories or feelings may arise, or that the client may feel uncomfortable or uneasy during the session. Therefore, it is important for the counselor to discuss these risks with the client and explain how they will be addressed if they arise.

Additionally, Christian counselors should obtain written consent from their clients before providing any counseling services. This written consent should clearly outline the scope of the counseling services being provided, including the duration of the counseling, the frequency of sessions, and the goals of the counseling. Furthermore, the written consent should also include a discussion of the client's rights, including the right to terminate counseling at any time and the right to have their records kept confidential.

Overall, obtaining informed consent is a crucial component of Christian counseling that helps to protect both the counselor and the client. By providing clients with detailed information about the counseling process and obtaining their written consent, counselors can ensure that clients are fully informed and empowered to make decisions about their own care.

Confidentiality

Maintaining confidentiality is an essential component of minimizing liability risk in Christian counseling. Christian counselors must ensure that all client information is kept confidential and secure, and that client information is only disclosed when legally required or with the client's written consent. To ensure that confidentiality is maintained, Christian counselors must take several steps. First, they should establish clear policies and procedures for maintaining confidentiality, including guidelines for when and how information may be disclosed. Second, they should conduct regular training sessions for all staff members, including office staff and interns, to ensure that everyone understands the importance of confidentiality and knows how to uphold it. Additionally, Christian counselors should invest in secure electronic storage systems and take precautions to ensure that all paper records are kept in a secure location. Finally, Christian counselors should take the time to develop strong relationships with their clients, actively listening to their needs and concerns and providing a safe and supportive environment where they feel comfortable sharing their thoughts and feelings. By taking these steps, Christian counselors can maintain confidentiality while providing effective and compassionate care to their clients.

Competent and Ethical Care

Providing competent and ethical care is crucial for minimizing liability risk in Christian counseling. To ensure the best possible outcomes for their clients, Christian counselors must be knowledgeable about evidence-based counseling techniques and best practices, as well as the unique challenges and opportunities presented by counseling from a Christian perspective. This may involve incorporating prayer or scripture into therapy sessions, or exploring the client's relationship with God or their faith community. Additionally, counselors must always strive to provide care that is consistent with Christian principles and values, such as compassion, empathy, and respect for human dignity.

To maintain a safe and healthy therapeutic relationship, counselors should establish and maintain appropriate boundaries with their clients. This includes setting clear expectations regarding confidentiality, avoiding dual relationships, and refraining from any behavior that could be seen as exploitative or abusive. It is also important for counselors to be aware of their own biases and limitations and to seek supervision or consultation as needed to ensure that they are providing the highest level of care possible.

10.3 Informed Consent in Christian Counseling

Obtaining informed consent is an essential part of providing effective and ethical care in Christian counseling. Informed consent involves providing clients with clear and comprehensive information about the nature of the counseling services, the potential risks and benefits, and their rights as clients. Christian counselors must ensure that clients are fully informed about the counseling process and have the opportunity to ask questions and seek clarification.

Elements of Informed Consent

Informed consent typically includes several key elements, including:

- A description of the counseling services that will be provided

- A discussion of the potential risks and benefits of counseling
- Information about the counselor's qualifications and experience
- A discussion of the counselor's fees and payment policies
- A description of the client's rights and responsibilities
- Information about confidentiality and the limits of confidentiality
- A discussion of any legal or ethical requirements that may impact the counseling process

Obtaining Informed Consent

Obtaining informed consent should be an ongoing process in Christian counseling. Christian counselors should provide clients with clear and comprehensive information about the counseling process and should encourage clients to ask questions and seek clarification. Counselors should also obtain written consent from their clients before providing any counseling services.

Challenges to Informed Consent

There are several challenges to obtaining informed consent in Christian counseling. For example, clients may have limited understanding of the counseling process or may be hesitant to share sensitive information with their counselor. In these situations, Christian counselors must take steps to ensure that clients have a clear understanding of the counseling process and feel comfortable sharing their experiences.

Another challenge to obtaining informed consent is ensuring that clients are fully informed about the potential risks and benefits of counseling. Christian counselors must be transparent about the potential risks and benefits of counseling and must ensure that clients have the information they need to make informed decisions about their care.

In conclusion, informed consent is a crucial aspect of providing effective and ethical care in Christian counseling. By providing clear and comprehensive information about the counseling process and obtaining written consent from clients, Christian counselors can ensure that clients are fully informed about their care and can make informed decisions about their mental health.

Chapter 11: Self-Care for Christian Counselors

11.1 Burnout and Compassion Fatigue in Christian Counseling

Signs and Symptoms of Burnout and Compassion Fatigue

It's important for Christian counselors to be aware of the signs and symptoms of burnout and compassion fatigue. Some of the most common indicators include:

- Feeling emotionally drained or numb
- Losing interest in work or other activities
- Feeling overwhelmed or helpless
- Experiencing physical symptoms, such as headaches or stomach problems
- Becoming irritable or easily angered
- Withdrawing from social interactions or isolating oneself

- Using alcohol or drugs to cope with stress
- Feeling a sense of cynicism or hopelessness about the future
- Struggling with feelings of guilt or shame

If left unaddressed, burnout and compassion fatigue can have serious consequences, both for the counselor and for their clients. Christian counselors who are experiencing symptoms of burnout or compassion fatigue should seek support and guidance from colleagues, supervisors, or mental health professionals.

Strategies for Preventing Burnout and Compassion Fatigue

Preventing burnout and compassion fatigue requires a proactive approach to self-care. Here are some strategies that Christian counselors can use to promote well-being and avoid burnout:

- Set healthy boundaries: Christian counselors should establish clear boundaries between their personal and professional lives, including setting limits on work hours, taking regular breaks, and prioritizing self-care activities.
- Engage in self-care activities: Engaging in activities that promote physical, emotional, and spiritual well-being can help Christian counselors reduce stress and prevent burnout. This may include exercise, mindfulness practices, spending time in nature, or engaging in creative hobbies.
- Seek support: Christian counselors should seek support from colleagues, supervisors, or mental health professionals when they are feeling overwhelmed or struggling with burnout or compassion fatigue. It's important to have a support network in place to help

manage stress and provide guidance and encouragement.

- Practice gratitude: Focusing on gratitude and positive experiences can help Christian counselors maintain a positive outlook and reduce feelings of burnout or compassion fatigue. This may involve keeping a gratitude journal or regularly reflecting on things that they are thankful for in their work and personal lives.
- Engage in ongoing education and training: Continuing education and training can help Christian counselors stay current on best practices in the field and feel confident in their ability to provide effective care. This can also help counselors feel more connected to their profession and reduce feelings of burnout or compassion fatigue.

Examples of Burnout and Compassion Fatigue in Christian Counseling

Here are some examples of situations that can lead to burnout and compassion fatigue in Christian counseling:

- A Christian counselor who works with survivors of trauma may experience burnout due to the intensity of the work and the emotional toll it takes on them.
- A Christian counselor who provides grief counseling may experience compassion fatigue as a result of hearing about clients' experiences of loss and trauma on a regular basis.
- A Christian counselor who works in a high-stress environment, such as a hospital or mental health clinic, may experience burnout due to the demands of the job and the need to manage a high caseload.
- A Christian counselor who takes on too many clients or works long hours may experience burnout due to the high levels of stress and emotional demands of the job.

- A Christian counselor who has difficulty establishing healthy boundaries with clients may experience burnout or compassion fatigue as a result of feeling overwhelmed or unable to manage their workload.

11.2 Strategies for Self-Care in Christian Counseling

There are several strategies that Christian counselors can use to promote self-care and prevent burnout and compassion fatigue. These include:

- Prioritizing Self-Care

  One of the most important strategies for preventing burnout and compassion fatigue is to prioritize self-care. This involves taking an active role in maintaining one's physical, emotional, and spiritual health. For example, Christian counselors may engage in regular exercise, practice meditation or mindfulness, or participate in activities that bring them joy and fulfillment.

- Setting Boundaries

  Setting boundaries is another key strategy for preventing burnout and compassion fatigue. Christian counselors must be mindful of their own limits and be willing to say no when necessary. This may involve setting limits on the number of clients seen each day or week, taking regular breaks throughout the day, or establishing clear policies and procedures for managing client emergencies.

- Seeking Support

Christian counselors should also seek support from colleagues, supervisors, and other professionals in the field. This may involve participating in peer support groups, seeking supervision or consultation, or attending professional development events. By connecting with others in the field, Christian counselors can gain valuable insights and support that can help them manage stress and avoid burnout.

- Engaging in Self-Reflection

Engaging in self-reflection is another important strategy for preventing burnout and compassion fatigue. Christian counselors should regularly reflect on their own emotional and mental state, as well as their interactions with clients. This may involve keeping a journal, engaging in regular self-assessments, or seeking feedback from colleagues or supervisors.

- Practicing Gratitude

Practicing gratitude is another effective strategy for promoting self-care and preventing burnout and compassion fatigue. Christian counselors should take time each day to reflect on the positive aspects of their work, such as the progress made by clients or the positive impact they have had on someone's life. By focusing on the positive, Christian counselors can maintain a sense of purpose and fulfillment in their work.

11.3 Supervision and Consultation in Christian Counseling

Supervision is a critical aspect of self-care for Christian counselors. It provides an opportunity for counselors to receive feedback, guidance, and support from a more experienced colleague or mentor. In Christian counseling, supervision may involve discussions about how to integrate faith and spirituality into the counseling process, and how to address issues related to religion and spirituality with clients.

The purpose of supervision is to help counselors develop their skills, reflect on their practice, and ensure that they are providing ethical and effective care to their clients. Supervisors may also help counselors address any personal issues or challenges that may be affecting their work.

Consultation in Christian Counseling

Consultation is another important aspect of self-care for Christian counselors. It involves seeking advice or guidance from colleagues or other professionals in the field. Consultation can be particularly helpful when counselors are dealing with complex cases or issues that are outside of their areas of expertise.

In Christian counseling, consultation may also involve seeking guidance on how to integrate faith and spirituality into the counseling process. This may include discussions about how to address issues related to sin, forgiveness, and salvation, and how to support clients who are struggling with issues of faith.

Engaging in supervision and consultation can provide a number of benefits for Christian counselors, including:

- Improved self-awareness and self-reflection
- Increased confidence and competence in counseling skills
- Enhanced ability to integrate faith and spirituality into the counseling process
- Increased ability to manage stress and prevent burnout
- Improved ability to provide ethical and effective care to clients

Examples of Supervision and Consultation in Christian Counseling

- Regular meetings with a supervisor or mentor to discuss cases, receive feedback, and reflect on practice
- Participating in peer consultation groups or professional organizations
- Seeking guidance from a trusted colleague or mentor when dealing with complex cases or ethical dilemmas
- Attending workshops or training sessions focused on developing counseling skills and integrating faith and spirituality into counseling practice.

Chapter 12: Assessment and Testing in Christian Counseling

Assessment and testing are crucial components of the Christian counseling process. They allow counselors to gather important information about their clients' mental health, well-being, and spiritual beliefs and practices. During the assessment, Christian counselors may use a variety of methods to evaluate their clients' strengths and weaknesses, including interviews, questionnaires, and psychological tests. Additionally, counselors may ask their clients to complete self-assessments to gain a better understanding of their personal experiences.

After the assessment, counselors can begin developing an effective treatment plan that addresses their clients' unique concerns. This plan may include a combination of approaches, such as talk therapy, cognitive-behavioral therapy, and spiritual counseling. By using a holistic approach that takes into account the physical, emotional, and spiritual needs of their clients, Christian counselors can help them achieve greater well-being and fulfillment in their lives.

Overall, assessment and testing play a critical role in the Christian counseling process. By gathering important information about their clients' needs and experiences, counselors can develop customized treatment plans that are tailored to each individual's unique situation. Through these efforts, Christian counselors can help their clients achieve greater emotional, mental, and spiritual health and well-being.

12.1 Psychological Testing in Christian Counseling

Psychological testing is an essential and valuable tool for Christian counselors. It provides them with objective measures of their clients' mental health and well-being, which is crucial in developing effective treatment plans.

These tests are specifically designed to assess a range of cognitive, emotional, and behavioral factors, and can be used to diagnose mental health disorders, assess personality traits, and evaluate the effectiveness of treatment. In addition, psychological testing can help counselors better understand their clients' strengths and weaknesses, identify areas of improvement, and tailor their counseling approach to meet their clients' specific needs. Furthermore, psychological testing can be used to monitor clients' progress and make any necessary adjustments to their treatment plan. Overall, the use of psychological testing in Christian counseling can lead to more accurate diagnoses, improved treatment outcomes, and better mental health and well-being for clients.

Types of Psychological Tests

There are various types of psychological tests that Christian counselors may use, including:

- Intelligence tests: These tests measure a person's cognitive abilities and intellectual potential.
- Personality tests: These tests assess a person's personality traits, such as extroversion, agreeableness, neuroticism, and conscientiousness.
- Neuropsychological tests: These tests evaluate a person's cognitive functioning, such as attention, memory, and language skills.
- Projective tests: These tests assess a person's unconscious thoughts and feelings by asking them to interpret ambiguous stimuli, such as inkblots or pictures.

Ethical Considerations

Christian counselors must be mindful of the ethical considerations involved in psychological testing, including issues related to confidentiality and informed consent. It is essential that clients understand the purpose and implications of the test and have given their informed consent to take it. Counselors should also be aware of the limitations of psychological testing and should use these assessments in conjunction with other sources of information, such as clinical interviews and client self-reports.

Benefits of Psychological Testing

Psychological testing is an incredibly useful tool for Christian counselors. It provides them with objective and standardized measures of their clients' mental health and well-being, allowing them to better understand their clients' needs and challenges. This understanding can then guide treatment planning and decision-making, leading to more effective and targeted interventions.

However, the benefits of psychological testing don't stop there. In addition to aiding in treatment planning, psychological testing can also help counselors evaluate the effectiveness of treatment over time. By periodically administering tests, counselors can track changes in their clients' mental health and well-being, as well as identify areas where further intervention may be necessary. This can help ensure that clients are receiving the care and support they need to improve their overall well-being.

Moreover, psychological testing can also provide valuable insight into a client's personality traits and behavioral patterns, which can be helpful in developing targeted treatment plans. By understanding a client's unique strengths and challenges, counselors can tailor their interventions to better meet their clients' needs, ultimately leading to more positive treatment outcomes.

In summary, psychological testing is an essential tool for Christian counselors. By providing objective and standardized measures of clients' mental health and well-being, it helps counselors to better understand their clients' needs and challenges. Furthermore, it can aid in treatment planning and decision-making, evaluate the effectiveness of treatment over time, and provide valuable insight into a client's personality traits and behavioral patterns.

Limitations of Psychological Testing

While psychological testing can be a useful tool for Christian counselors, it is not without its limitations. It is important to keep in mind that these tests are not perfect, and their results must be interpreted within the context of other information gathered during the counseling process. Furthermore, psychological tests can be influenced by a variety of factors, including the client's emotional state, motivation, and cultural background.

Conclusion

Overall, psychological testing is a valuable tool for Christian counselors, providing them with important information about their clients' mental health and well-being. By using these assessments in conjunction with other sources of information and being mindful of the ethical considerations involved, Christian counselors can provide more effective and ethical care to their clients.

12.2 Assessment of Spiritual Well-Being in Christian Counseling

Assessment of spiritual well-being is an important component of Christian counseling, as it recognizes that spirituality is an integral part of human experience and can play a significant role in mental health and well-being. Christian counselors need to assess their clients' spiritual beliefs, practices, and experiences as part of the overall assessment process. This involves a comprehensive evaluation of the client's beliefs and behaviors, including religious affiliation, spiritual practices, and experiences of transcendent states.

Importance of Spiritual Assessment

Assessment of spiritual well-being is an essential aspect of Christian counseling. It provides counselors with a comprehensive understanding of their clients' needs and concerns. By examining the client's spiritual health, counselors can gain greater insight into the impact of their faith on their mental health. This information is especially important for clients who seek out Christian counselors to integrate their faith into the counseling process. Clients who share religious beliefs with their counselors may feel more comfortable discussing their spiritual experiences, which can provide valuable information for treatment.

Furthermore, spiritual well-being can be a crucial component of mental health problems. Identifying and addressing spiritual issues can lead to better outcomes for clients. By assessing spiritual well-being, Christian counselors can develop more effective treatment plans that address the root causes of their clients' mental health issues. This may involve exploring the client's beliefs and values, examining their relationship with God, and identifying areas of spiritual growth.

In conclusion, assessing spiritual well-being is a vital component of Christian counseling. It allows counselors to gain a deeper understanding of their clients' needs and concerns, which can lead to more effective treatment. By examining spiritual factors, Christian counselors can help clients integrate their faith into the counseling process and address the root causes of their mental health issues.

Methods of Spiritual Assessment

There are a variety of methods that Christian counselors can use to assess spiritual well-being. These include standardized measures, clinical interviews, and client self-reports.

Standardized Measures

Standardized measures of spiritual well-being have been developed and validated to assess a wide range of spiritual constructs. These measures provide a more structured and objective approach to assessment and can be useful in research and clinical practice. They are designed to gauge an individual's spiritual health, as well as identify areas of strength and potential growth. By using standardized measures of spiritual well-being, researchers and clinicians can gain a more comprehensive understanding of a person's spiritual life and how it affects their overall health and well-being.

Some examples of commonly used standardized measures of spiritual well-being include:

- Spiritual Well-Being Scale: This scale measures an individual's sense of purpose and meaning in life, as well as their sense of connection to a higher power or force.
- Brief Multidimensional Measure of Religiousness/Spirituality: This measure assesses an individual's religious and spiritual beliefs, practices, and experiences.
- Daily Spiritual Experiences Scale: This scale measures an individual's daily experiences of spiritual connection and transcendence.
- Index of Core Spiritual Experiences: This measure assesses an individual's core spiritual experiences, including feelings of awe, transcendence, and inner peace.

Overall, using standardized measures of spiritual well-being can provide valuable insights into an individual's spiritual life and how it relates to their overall health and well-being.

Clinical Interviews

Clinical interviews are a crucial component in assessing the spiritual well-being of clients. Conducting clinical interviews allows Christian counselors to gain more insight into their clients' unique spiritual beliefs, practices, and experiences. Additionally, the interviews provide a more individualized and contextualized approach to spiritual well-being assessment.

When conducting clinical interviews, it is essential to explore a range of key areas. One critical area to explore is the client's religious or spiritual affiliation and history. This information can provide valuable context for understanding the client's spiritual beliefs and practices. Another important area to explore is the client's spiritual practices and rituals. By exploring these practices, counselors can gain insight into the client's spiritual well-being, including areas of strength and potential areas for growth.

Another critical area to explore in clinical interviews is the client's experience of a higher power or transcendent states. This area can be particularly important for clients who have experienced trauma or significant life changes, as it can offer a sense of comfort and support. It is also crucial to explore the client's religious or spiritual coping mechanisms. This information can provide insights into how the client copes with stressors and challenges in their life.

Lastly, it is important to explore any spiritual struggles or doubts that the client may be experiencing. These struggles can be an indicator of areas where the client may need additional support or guidance. By exploring these areas, counselors can gain a more comprehensive understanding of their clients' spiritual well-being, which can inform their treatment approach and ultimately lead to better outcomes.

Client Self-Reports

Christian counselors can use client self-reports to assess spiritual well-being. This can be a valuable tool for understanding clients' experiences and beliefs in their own words and can provide unique insights into their spiritual lives. Some examples of client self-reports that Christian counselors can use to assess spiritual well-being include:

- Daily spiritual experience scale: This scale measures the frequency and intensity of spiritual experiences that clients have on a daily basis. It can help clients identify

- patterns in their spiritual experiences and assess the impact of these experiences on their well-being.
- Religious and spiritual struggles scale: This scale measures the degree to which clients experience conflicts or doubts related to their religious or spiritual beliefs. It can help clients explore these struggles and find ways to resolve them.
- Spiritual Transcendence Scale: This scale measures the degree to which clients experience a sense of connection to something greater than themselves. It can help clients explore their sense of purpose and meaning in life and find ways to connect with something larger than themselves.
- Intrinsic Spirituality Scale: This scale measures the degree to which clients feel connected to their inner selves or personal spirituality. It can help clients explore their sense of identity and values and find ways to cultivate a deeper sense of self-awareness and self-acceptance.

In addition to these self-reports, Christian counselors can also use a variety of other assessment tools to evaluate spiritual well-being, including interviews, observations, and standardized measures. By gathering information from multiple sources, Christian counselors can develop a more comprehensive understanding of their clients' spiritual lives and tailor their counseling approach accordingly.

Overall, assessing spiritual well-being is an important aspect of Christian counseling that can help clients find deeper meaning, purpose, and fulfillment in their lives. By exploring their spiritual beliefs and experiences, clients can gain a greater sense of connection to themselves, others, and God, and can find new ways to cope with life's challenges and uncertainties.

Christian counselors have an important responsibility to be mindful of the ethical considerations that come with assessing spiritual well-being. It is crucial to be aware of issues related to informed consent, confidentiality, and cultural competence. One way to achieve this is by ensuring that clients are fully informed about the purpose and scope of the assessment, and that they understand how the results will be used in treatment. In addition, it is important for Christian counselors to possess the necessary skills and knowledge to conduct spiritual assessments in a culturally competent and sensitive manner. This includes respecting and accommodating clients' diverse spiritual beliefs and practices. Failure to do so can undermine the integrity of the counseling relationship and hinder the client's progress toward achieving their goals. To achieve cultural competence, Christian counselors should be knowledgeable about different cultural practices and beliefs, and be able to adapt their methods to the client's unique needs. Practicing sensitivity and empathy can go a long way in providing a safe and supportive environment for the client to share their spiritual experiences. Additionally, counselors should be aware of the limitations of their knowledge and seek to learn more about different cultures and beliefs. This can help counselors to identify and address any blind spots they may have, and ultimately improve their effectiveness in delivering high-quality care.

Conclusion

Assessment of spiritual well-being is a critical component of effective and ethical Christian counseling. By using a variety of assessment methods, Christian counselors can gain a deeper understanding of their client's spiritual needs and develop more effective treatment plans. Christian counselors must be aware of the ethical considerations involved in the assessment of spiritual well-being and should ensure that they are conducting assessments in a culturally competent and sensitive manner.

12.3 Cultural Competence in Assessment and Testing

Christian counselors must understand that cultural competence is essential for effective assessment and testing. The cultural background of a client can greatly influence their worldview, values, and beliefs, and these factors can impact their mental health and well-being. Counselors need to be aware of these differences and understand the ways in which culture can impact the assessment and testing process.

Cultural competence also involves the recognition and respect of the diversity within a given culture. For example, two individuals from the same racial or ethnic background may have very different experiences and beliefs based on their individual experiences and perspectives. Christian counselors must be sensitive to these differences and avoid making assumptions about their clients based on cultural stereotypes.

Culturally Sensitive Assessment Tools and Techniques

To promote cultural competence in assessment and testing, Christian counselors should be familiar with culturally sensitive assessment tools and techniques. These tools should be designed to be culturally relevant and should consider the client's cultural background when evaluating their mental health and well-being.

For example, some assessment tools may be biased toward Western cultural values, and may not be appropriate for use with clients from non-Western backgrounds. Christian counselors should be aware of these potential biases and should seek out culturally appropriate assessments that can provide more accurate and relevant information about their clients.

Christian counselors should be willing to adapt their assessments to meet the unique needs of their clients. This may involve modifying the assessment process to accommodate different cultural beliefs or practices, or it may involve selecting a different assessment tool altogether.

For example, in some cultures, it may be considered inappropriate to discuss personal issues with strangers or to disclose personal information. In these cases, Christian counselors may need to modify their assessment process to allow for a more gradual disclosure of information and to build trust with their clients over time.

Christian counselors should also be aware of the potential biases and limitations of standardized assessments. These assessments are designed to be administered and scored in a standardized way, and may not take into account individual cultural differences.

Additionally, some standardized assessments may have limitations in their ability to accurately diagnose mental health disorders in certain populations. For example, some assessments may not be appropriate for use with clients

153

from non-Western cultures, or may not be sensitive to the experiences of LGBTQ+ individuals.

Christian counselors should use multiple sources of information to ensure that their assessments are accurate and culturally sensitive. In addition to standardized assessments, counselors should also conduct clinical interviews and gather information from client self-reports.

By using multiple sources of information, Christian counselors can gain a more comprehensive understanding of their clients' needs, and can develop treatment plans that are tailored to their unique concerns and cultural backgrounds.

Examples of Culturally Sensitive Assessment Tools

- The Multicultural Counseling Inventory is a tool that is designed to assess cultural competence and sensitivity in counseling.
- The Acculturation Rating Scale for Mexican Americans assesses the level of acculturation of Mexican Americans and their orientation to both Mexican and American cultures.
- The Culture-Free Self-Esteem Inventory is a tool that is designed to assess self-esteem in a way that is free from cultural bias.
- The Black Racial Identity Scale is a tool that assesses the racial identity development of African Americans.
- The Sexual Orientation Counselor Competency Scale is a tool that assesses the competency of counselors working with LGBTQ+ individuals.

In conclusion, promoting cultural competence in the assessment and testing process is crucial for effective and compassionate Christian counseling. By being aware of the cultural factors that can impact mental health and well-being, using culturally sensitive assessment tools and techniques, and adapting assessments to meet the unique needs of their clients, Christian counselors can provide more accurate and relevant care to clients from diverse cultural backgrounds.

Chapter 13: Christian Counseling and Mental Health

13.1 Common Mental Health Disorders in Christian Counseling

Mental health disorders are prevalent in our society and Christian counselors may encounter individuals struggling with various mental health disorders. It is important for Christian counselors to be aware of the common mental health disorders that they may encounter, so that they can provide appropriate care and support to their clients. In this section, we will discuss some of the most common mental health disorders that Christian counselors may encounter.

Depression

Depression is a common mental health disorder that can cause persistent feelings of sadness, loss of interest in activities, and other symptoms that can interfere with daily life. Depression can occur due to various reasons including genetic factors, life experiences, and environmental factors. Common symptoms of depression include:

- Persistent feelings of sadness or emptiness
- Loss of interest in activities
- Changes in appetite or weight
- Insomnia or hypersomnia
- Fatigue or loss of energy
- Feelings of worthlessness or guilt
- Difficulty concentrating or making decisions
- Thoughts of death or suicide

Christian counselors must be aware of the signs and symptoms of depression and be prepared to provide appropriate care and support to their clients.

Anxiety

Anxiety disorders are characterized by persistent feelings of worry and fear that can interfere with daily life. These disorders can take many forms, including generalized anxiety disorder, panic disorder, and social anxiety disorder. Anxiety disorders can occur due to various reasons including genetic factors, life experiences, and environmental factors. Common symptoms of anxiety disorders include:

- Persistent feelings of worry or fear
- Panic attacks
- Avoidance of social situations or activities
- Irrational fears or phobias
- Physical symptoms such as heart palpitations, sweating, and trembling

Christian counselors must be aware of the signs and symptoms of anxiety disorders and be prepared to provide appropriate care and support to their clients.

Post-Traumatic Stress Disorder (PTSD)

PTSD is a mental health disorder that can develop after a person experiences or witnesses a traumatic event. Symptoms can include flashbacks, nightmares, and severe anxiety. PTSD can occur due to various reasons including experiencing or witnessing a traumatic event such as war, natural disasters, or physical and sexual abuse. Common symptoms of PTSD include:

- Flashbacks of the traumatic event
- Avoidance of reminders of the traumatic event
- Hyperarousal or hypervigilance
- Nightmares or intrusive thoughts
- Difficulty sleeping or concentrating

Christian counselors must be aware of the signs and symptoms of PTSD and be prepared to provide appropriate care and support to their clients.

Substance Abuse

Substance abuse is a common problem among clients seeking Christian counseling. Substance abuse can cause a range of problems, including physical health problems, legal issues, and interpersonal conflicts. Substance abuse can occur due to various reasons including social and environmental factors, genetic factors, and coping mechanisms. Common symptoms of substance abuse include:

- Continued use of substances despite negative consequences
- Difficulty controlling substance use
- Tolerance and withdrawal symptoms
- Neglecting responsibilities and obligations
- Interpersonal problems

Christian counselors must be aware of the signs and symptoms of substance abuse and be prepared to provide appropriate care and support to their clients.

Eating Disorders

Eating disorders are serious mental health disorders that can have significant impacts on physical health, emotional well-being, and social functioning. Eating disorders can occur due to various reasons including genetic factors, social and environmental factors, and psychological factors. Common eating disorders include:

- Anorexia nervosa: characterized by extreme weight loss, fear of gaining weight, and distorted body image
- Bulimia nervosa: characterized by binge eating and compensatory behaviors such as vomiting or excessive exercise
- Binge-eating disorder: characterized by recurrent episodes of overeating without compensatory behaviors

Christian counselors must be knowledgeable about these disorders and their treatment options, as well as the potential spiritual implications of mental health issues. In addition to providing clinical interventions, Christian counselors may also incorporate prayer, meditation, and other spiritual practices into their treatment plans.

It's important to note that mental health disorders can affect individuals from all walks of life, regardless of their faith or religious background. Christian counselors must be able to provide non-judgmental and compassionate care to all clients, regardless of their beliefs or lifestyle choices.

Importance of Accurate Diagnosis

Accurate diagnosis is essential for the effective treatment of mental health disorders in Christian counseling. A proper diagnosis can help counselors develop an appropriate treatment plan that addresses the client's specific needs. To ensure an accurate diagnosis, Christian counselors may use a combination of clinical assessments, psychological testing, and client self-reports.

It's also important for Christian counselors to be aware of the potential for misdiagnosis, particularly for disorders that may present with symptoms that are similar to spiritual experiences, such as religious or mystical experiences. In such cases, counselors may need to use specialized assessment tools or seek consultation from other professionals to ensure an accurate diagnosis.

Importance of Holistic Treatment

In Christian counseling, holistic treatment is often emphasized, meaning that clients are treated as whole persons with physical, emotional, social, and spiritual needs. This approach recognizes the interconnectedness of these domains and the potential impact that spiritual well-being can have on mental health.

Holistic treatment may involve a variety of interventions, including medication, therapy, and lifestyle changes, as well as spiritual practices such as prayer, meditation, and scripture study. Christian counselors may also incorporate elements of Christian theology and spirituality into their treatment plans to help clients find meaning, purpose, and hope in their struggles.

In some cases, Christian counselors may need to refer clients to other professionals for specialized treatment or evaluation. Referral may be necessary when a client's needs exceed the scope of the counselor's training and expertise or when a client requires medical or psychiatric intervention.

Referral should be done in a compassionate and supportive manner, with the client's best interests in mind. Christian counselors should work collaboratively with other professionals to ensure that clients receive the best possible care.

Here are some additional examples of mental health disorders that Christian counselors may encounter in their work:

- Bipolar disorder: Bipolar disorder is a mental health disorder characterized by extreme mood swings, ranging from manic episodes to depressive episodes.
- Obsessive-compulsive disorder (OCD): OCD is a mental health disorder characterized by persistent and intrusive thoughts or behaviors that can interfere with daily life.
- Borderline personality disorder: Borderline personality disorder is a mental health disorder characterized by unstable moods, behavior, and relationships.

- Eating disorders: Eating disorders are mental health disorders characterized by unhealthy relationships with food and body image, including anorexia, bulimia, and binge-eating disorder.

Christian counselors must be knowledgeable about these disorders and their treatment options and must be able to provide compassionate and effective care to clients who may be struggling with these and other mental health concerns.

13.2 Medication and Christian Counseling

Medication can be an important part of managing mental health disorders for some clients, and Christian counselors may encounter clients who are taking medication to manage their symptoms. While Christian counselors are not authorized to prescribe medication, they should be knowledgeable about the benefits and risks of medication and should be able to provide appropriate support and guidance to clients who are taking medication.

Benefits and Risks of Medication

It is important for Christian counselors to understand the benefits and risks of medication as a treatment option for mental health disorders. Some benefits of medication may include:

- Reducing symptoms of mental health disorders
- Improving the quality of life
- Enhancing overall functioning
- Preventing relapse

However, there are also potential risks and side effects associated with medication use, which can vary depending on the specific medication and the individual client. Some risks of medication use may include:

- Physical side effects, such as weight gain, nausea, or fatigue
- Risk of addiction or dependence on medication
- Interference with spiritual practices or beliefs
- Limited effectiveness for some individuals

Supporting Clients Who Are Taking Medication

Christian counselors should be able to provide support and guidance to clients who are taking medication for mental health disorders. This may include:

- Educating clients on the benefits and risks of medication use
- Helping clients understand their medication regimen, including dosage and potential side effects
- Encouraging clients to communicate with their medical providers about their medication use and any concerns or issues that arise
- Providing emotional support and helping clients manage any spiritual conflicts or concerns related to medication use

Working with Medical Professionals

Christian counselors should also be able to work with medical professionals, such as psychiatrists or primary care physicians, to ensure that clients are receiving appropriate care and support. This may involve:

- Communicating with medical professionals to understand the client's medication regimen and any potential interactions or concerns
- Encouraging clients to communicate with their medical providers and to attend regular appointments
- Collaborating with medical professionals to develop a comprehensive treatment plan that incorporates both medication and counseling

Examples of Medications Used to Treat Mental Health Disorders

Some common medications used to treat mental health disorders include:

- Selective serotonin reuptake inhibitors (SSRIs): used to treat depression, anxiety, and some other mental health disorders
- Benzodiazepines: used to treat anxiety and panic disorders
- Antipsychotics: used to treat schizophrenia and other psychotic disorders
- Mood stabilizers: used to treat bipolar disorder
- Stimulants: used to treat attention deficit hyperactivity disorder (ADHD)

It is important for Christian counselors to understand the potential benefits and risks of these medications and to be knowledgeable about their appropriate use and potential side effects.

13.3 Referring Clients for Mental Health Treatment

Integrating faith and mental health treatment is a core component of Christian counseling. Christian counselors must be able to effectively integrate the client's spiritual beliefs and practices into the counseling process to provide holistic care. Here are some key considerations for integrating faith and mental health treatment:

The first step in integrating faith and mental health treatment is to ensure a comprehensive understanding of the client's spiritual beliefs. Christian counselors should be vigilant about their own biases and assumptions, and be willing to engage in respectful dialogue with clients about their beliefs. The counselor should take time to discuss the client's religious background, their current spiritual practices, and their beliefs about the role of faith in mental health treatment. Additionally, the counselor should encourage the client to explore the different aspects of their spirituality and how it impacts their mental health. This can include having the client describe their experiences with prayer, meditation or other spiritual practices. By understanding the client's spiritual perspective, the counselor can better tailor treatment and interventions to the client's needs. It is important to note that while Christian counselors may have a specific set of beliefs, they should not impose their beliefs on the client. Rather, the counselor should help the client to explore their own spirituality in a safe and supportive environment.

Incorporating Scripture and Prayer

Christian counselors can incorporate scripture and prayer into the counseling process to support clients in their spiritual journey. This can include sharing relevant Bible verses, encouraging clients to engage in prayer and meditation, and exploring how clients can draw on their faith to cope with mental health challenges.

Additionally, Christian counselors can use their faith to help clients find meaning and purpose in their lives. They can assist clients in exploring their values, developing a sense of identity, and discovering their unique calling. By integrating spiritual principles into counseling sessions, Christian counselors can help clients achieve a deeper sense of fulfillment and purpose.

Furthermore, Christian counselors can help clients improve their relationships with others by drawing on biblical teachings on forgiveness, compassion, and love. They can guide clients in developing healthier communication skills, resolving conflicts, and fostering positive connections with friends and family members.

In summary, Christian counseling offers a holistic approach to mental health that incorporates clients' spiritual beliefs and values. By integrating scripture and prayer into the counseling process, Christian counselors can help clients find meaning and purpose in their lives, develop healthier relationships, and cope with mental health challenges in a way that aligns with their faith.

Collaborating with Spiritual Leaders

Christian counselors can have a wide range of ways to collaborate with their clients' spiritual leaders, such as pastors or other clergy members, in order to support their clients' spiritual well-being, as well as their mental health. For instance, they can refer clients to their spiritual leaders for additional support and guidance or they can work together with spiritual leaders to develop a comprehensive treatment plan that integrates both spiritual and mental health care. Additionally, Christian counselors can also provide clients with useful resources, such as books, podcasts, or online materials, which can complement the work they are doing with their spiritual leaders. They can also create a safe and supportive environment where clients can explore their own spirituality and find their own meaning and purpose in life. Ultimately, Christian counselors are committed to helping their clients grow and thrive in all aspects of their lives, including their spiritual and emotional well-being.

One of the key challenges in integrating faith and mental health treatment is balancing clients' spiritual and psychological needs. Christian counselors must be able to navigate this delicate balance and be willing to adapt their approach to meet the unique needs of each client.

To achieve this balance, Christian counselors need to have a strong foundation in both spiritual and psychological aspects of counseling. They should have a deep understanding of the client's unique religious and cultural background, as well as the psychological theories and techniques that are most effective in addressing their particular mental health concerns.

In addition to this, Christian counselors must be prepared to face the challenges that arise when integrating faith and psychology. They must be willing to navigate the complexities of the therapeutic relationship, such as boundaries, confidentiality, and ethical considerations, in a way that is consistent with their faith and values.

Overall, while integrating faith and mental health treatment can be challenging, Christian counselors who are willing to put in the time and effort to develop their skills and understanding of both spiritual and psychological aspects of counseling can provide truly holistic care that meets the unique needs of each client.

Here are some examples of how Christian counselors can integrate faith and mental health treatment:

- Using scripture to support clients who are struggling with feelings of guilt or shame
- Encouraging clients to engage in prayer and meditation to manage anxiety or depression symptoms
- Collaborating with spiritual leaders to provide support to clients who are struggling with spiritual crises or doubts
- Incorporating spiritual practices, such as journaling or mindfulness, into the counseling process to support clients' spiritual and mental health needs
- Supporting clients who are grappling with existential questions, such as the meaning of life or the role of suffering, through discussions of theology and faith.

In conclusion, integrating faith and mental health treatment is a key component of Christian counseling. By understanding the client's spiritual beliefs, incorporating scripture and prayer, collaborating with spiritual leaders, balancing spiritual and psychological needs, and providing support that integrates both spiritual and mental health care, Christian counselors can provide holistic care that supports clients' overall well-being.

Chapter 14: Intersectionality in Christian Counseling

14.1 Addressing Issues of Race and Ethnicity in Christian Counseling

Christian counselors must be aware of the impact of race and ethnicity on mental health and well-being. They must be prepared to address issues related to cultural identity, discrimination, and social justice in their work with clients from diverse racial and ethnic backgrounds. In addition, it is important for counselors to recognize that cultural factors such as family dynamics, religious beliefs, and socioeconomic status can also play a significant role in a person's mental health. Therefore, counselors should strive to develop a deep understanding of the cultural backgrounds of their clients in order to provide effective and culturally sensitive therapy. Moreover, counselors must also be aware of the unique challenges faced by individuals who belong to marginalized communities, including the LGBTQ+ community, people with disabilities, and those living in poverty. By understanding and addressing these issues, Christian counselors can provide more comprehensive and effective care to their clients, ultimately helping them achieve greater mental and emotional well-being.

One of the key challenges in addressing issues of race and ethnicity in Christian counseling is acknowledging and addressing the ways in which racism and discrimination can impact mental health. Christian counselors must be prepared to engage in difficult conversations with clients about their experiences of racism, prejudice, and discrimination, and to help clients develop coping strategies to manage the impact of these experiences on their mental health.

As the world becomes increasingly diverse, it is important for Christian counselors to remain aware of the ways in which race and ethnicity can affect individuals' experiences and perspectives. In order to provide effective counseling, it is necessary to understand the unique challenges faced by people of different backgrounds, and to approach clients with sensitivity and empathy.

Furthermore, it is important to recognize that the impact of racism and discrimination is not limited to individuals who have personally experienced it. Even those who have not experienced racism or discrimination themselves may still be affected by it, either as witnesses to others' experiences or through exposure to media coverage of incidents of racism and discrimination.

Given these complexities, Christian counselors must be prepared to approach the issue of race and ethnicity in counseling with nuance and sensitivity. This may involve ongoing education and training to stay up-to-date on issues related to diversity and inclusion, as well as a willingness to listen to and learn from clients' experiences. Ultimately, by acknowledging and addressing the impact of racism and discrimination on mental health, Christian counselors can help clients to achieve greater wellbeing and resilience in the face of adversity.

Utilizing Culturally Sensitive Assessment Tools

Christian counselors can use a wide range of culturally sensitive assessment tools and techniques to gain a more nuanced understanding of the unique needs and experiences of clients from diverse racial and ethnic backgrounds. In order to better serve African American or Latino clients, for example, counselors may choose to use specialized assessments that are tailored to the specific cultural backgrounds of these groups. Additionally, counselors may opt to use assessment tools that are designed to be culturally sensitive and free from bias, so that they can impartially assess the needs of clients from all backgrounds. By using these tools, counselors can ensure that they are providing the most effective and compassionate care possible to all of their clients, regardless of their cultural background.

Incorporating Cultural Competency into Treatment Plans

Christian counselors may also consider incorporating additional elements of cultural competency into their treatment plans. They may explore the cultural values and beliefs of their clients in greater depth, and utilize a wider range of culturally specific interventions to help them better connect with their clients. Additionally, counselors may consider adapting their treatment plans to meet the unique needs of clients from diverse cultural backgrounds. This could include addressing language barriers or incorporating culturally relevant materials into therapy sessions. By taking a more culturally sensitive approach, counselors can help their clients feel more understood and supported on their journey towards healing.

Christian counselors play a crucial role in addressing the unique challenges that clients from diverse racial and ethnic backgrounds face. In addition to the traditional counseling tasks, such as offering guidance and support, Christian counselors must also be prepared to deal with issues related to social justice. This includes addressing systemic oppression and inequality, advocating for clients' rights and needs, and working to promote social change. Through their work, Christian counselors have the opportunity to promote healing and transformation not only in individual lives, but also in whole communities. By fostering understanding, compassion, and respect, they can help to break down barriers and build bridges between people of different races and ethnicities, making our world a more just and equitable place for all.

Examples of issues related to race and ethnicity that may arise in Christian counseling include:

- A client who has experienced discrimination in the workplace and is struggling with feelings of anger and frustration
- A client who is a member of a marginalized racial or ethnic group and is experiencing symptoms of depression as a result of systemic oppression and discrimination
- A client who is struggling to reconcile their cultural identity with their faith, and is seeking guidance on how to navigate this process

- A client who has experienced trauma related to racial or ethnic violence, and is seeking support in coping with the psychological impact of this trauma.

14.2 Socioeconomic Status and Christian Counseling

Socioeconomic status, or the measure of an individual's or household's economic and social position based on income, education, and occupation, can have a substantial effect on mental health and well-being. For example, individuals with lower socioeconomic status may experience higher levels of stress, depression, and anxiety due to financial instability, limited access to healthcare, and other economic challenges. Moreover, these individuals may experience social exclusion and discrimination, which can further exacerbate mental health issues. Thus, it is crucial for Christian counselors to be equipped with the necessary skills and knowledge to address these complex issues related to poverty, unemployment, and other economic challenges in their work with clients. This may include creating a safe and non-judgmental space for clients to share their experiences, providing practical resources and support, and advocating for policies that promote social and economic equality. By doing so, Christian counselors can play a critical role in promoting the mental health and well-being of individuals from all socioeconomic backgrounds.

Understanding the Impact of Socioeconomic Status on Mental Health

The impact of socioeconomic status on mental health is a complex issue that requires Christian counselors to be equipped with the necessary skills and knowledge to address these challenges. Poverty, unemployment, and financial instability can all contribute to poor mental health outcomes, including depression, anxiety, and stress. However, it is important to recognize that the impact of socioeconomic status on mental health is not limited to financial strain.

For example, individuals with low socioeconomic status may experience social exclusion and discrimination, which can further exacerbate mental health issues. Moreover, research has shown that social support, access to resources, and education level can all play a role in mental health outcomes. Therefore, Christian counselors must take a holistic approach to their clients' mental health and consider a range of factors that may be impacting their well-being.

Christian counselors must also be aware of the unique challenges that individuals from diverse socioeconomic backgrounds can face. For example, individuals from low-income backgrounds may face barriers to mental health services, including lack of transportation or limited access to mental health providers in their area. Moreover, they may also experience stigma around seeking mental health services, which can further prevent them from seeking help.

To address these challenges, Christian counselors must be prepared to work with their clients to develop strategies for managing financial stress and connecting them with resources that can provide financial assistance. Additionally, counselors can provide support and guidance to clients who may be experiencing job loss or financial instability. By taking a proactive approach to addressing socioeconomic challenges, Christian counselors can help their clients achieve greater well-being and resilience in the face of these difficult circumstances.

Furthermore, Christian counselors can also engage in
advocacy and social justice work to address the systemic
issues that contribute to economic inequality and poverty.
This may involve advocating for policies and programs that
support economic mobility and opportunity, as well as
addressing the impact of racism and discrimination on
economic outcomes.

In summary, socioeconomic status can have a significant
impact on mental health outcomes, and it is important for
Christian counselors to be equipped with the necessary
skills and knowledge to address these challenges. By taking
a comprehensive approach to mental health and considering
a range of factors that may be impacting their clients' well-
being, Christian counselors can help their clients achieve
greater resilience and well-being in the face of challenging
socioeconomic circumstances.

Addressing the Practical Challenges of Economic Hardship

Christian counselors must also be prepared to help clients
address the practical challenges that often come with
economic hardship. The first step in this process is to
establish a trusting relationship with the client. Once trust
has been established, the counselor can work with the client
to identify specific areas where they may need assistance.
This may include working with clients to develop strategies
for managing debt, such as creating a budget and
prioritizing expenses. The counselor can also assist clients
in accessing affordable housing and healthcare, and can
help them build financial literacy and job skills through
vocational training programs or educational courses. By
addressing these practical challenges, Christian counselors
can help their clients achieve a greater sense of stability and
security, which can lead to improved mental and emotional
well-being.

In addition to addressing the immediate practical and psychological impacts of economic hardship, Christian counselors may also engage in advocacy and social justice work to address the systemic issues that contribute to economic inequality and poverty. This may include not only advocating for policies and programs that support economic mobility and opportunity, but also researching the root causes of economic inequality and poverty in order to better understand how to combat these issues. Christian counselors may also work on addressing the impact of racism and discrimination on economic outcomes by partnering with organizations that work to eliminate systemic racism and by educating their clients on the ways in which racism and discrimination can impact economic well-being. Furthermore, Christian counselors may work to provide financial education and resources to their clients, helping them to develop the skills and knowledge necessary to achieve economic stability and success. By addressing both the immediate and systemic issues related to economic hardship, Christian counselors can play an important role in promoting economic justice and equality in their communities.

Utilizing Community Resources

Christian counselors can be a valuable resource for clients who are facing economic challenges. In addition to providing emotional support and guidance, they can also help clients connect with a variety of community resources. For example, they may have information about local food banks and other programs that can help clients meet their basic needs. They may also be able to provide guidance on financial assistance programs that can help with rent, utilities, and other expenses. In some cases, Christian counselors may even be able to help clients find job training and placement services that can help them improve their financial situation in the long term. By drawing on these resources, Christian counselors can provide comprehensive support for clients who are facing economic difficulties.

When working with clients from diverse cultural backgrounds, Christian counselors must also be aware of the ways in which cultural values and beliefs may shape attitudes toward wealth and poverty, as well as the impact of systemic racism and discrimination on economic outcomes.

It is important to note that economic outcomes are often shaped by a complex interplay of factors, including access to education, job opportunities, and systemic barriers to upward mobility. Christian counselors can play an important role in helping clients navigate these challenges, by providing resources and support that are tailored to the unique needs of each individual.

Culturally sensitive approaches can be particularly effective in engaging clients in discussions about economic challenges. By acknowledging and respecting the diversity of experiences and perspectives among clients, counselors can create a safe and supportive environment that encourages open and honest dialogue.

Moreover, developing strategies for addressing economic challenges in a culturally responsive way requires a deep understanding of the client's cultural context. This may involve exploring traditional cultural practices and beliefs related to wealth and poverty, as well as the impact of historical and contemporary social and economic policies on the client's community. Christian counselors can work collaboratively with clients to identify strategies that are consistent with their values and beliefs, and that take into account the unique challenges that they face.

Examples of Christian Counseling Interventions for Addressing Socioeconomic Challenges

- Developing financial management and budgeting skills with clients
- Connecting clients with community resources such as job training programs, food banks, and financial assistance programs
- Advocating for policies and programs that address economic inequality and promote economic mobility
- Addressing the impact of racism and discrimination on economic outcomes
- Providing support and guidance to clients who may be experiencing job loss or financial instability
- Incorporating elements of social justice and advocacy into counseling sessions to address the root causes of economic hardship.

14.3 Gender and Christian Counseling

Gender is a multifaceted and complex aspect of identity that can have a significant impact on mental health and well-being. It is an internal sense that an individual has of their gender, and can manifest in various ways, including gender expression. Gender expression is the outward manifestation of one's gender identity and can encompass many different aspects such as dress, mannerisms, and behavior.

In addition to these aspects, gender can also be affected by societal norms and expectations, which can lead to experiences of sexism and gender-based violence. These experiences can have a profound impact on mental health and well-being, and can contribute to feelings of anxiety, depression, and other mental health issues. Therefore, it is important that we strive to create a world in which people of all genders are treated with equal respect and dignity, and where gender-based discrimination and violence are not tolerated.

Christian counselors play an important role in providing effective care to clients. To do so, it is crucial that they have a solid understanding of gender identity and expression. This includes recognizing that gender is a spectrum and that individuals may identify as male, female, non-binary, or any other gender identity that reflects their own personal experience.

However, it is important to note that gender identity is just one aspect of a person's identity and should not be viewed in isolation. Christian counselors must be mindful of the intersectionality between gender identity and other factors such as race, ethnicity, religion, and sexual orientation.

To provide effective care, counselors must also recognize that gender expression can vary greatly between individuals and cultures, and may include factors such as clothing, hairstyles, and mannerisms. By engaging in open and non-judgmental conversations with clients about their gender identity and expression, counselors can create a safe and inclusive environment for clients to explore and express themselves. This can lead to greater self-awareness, self-acceptance, and ultimately, greater emotional well-being.

Gender-based violence is a pervasive issue that can have a profound impact on the mental health and well-being of survivors. This can manifest in a multitude of ways, including anxiety, depression, and post-traumatic stress disorder (PTSD). As Christian counselors, it is important to understand the complex nature of gender-based violence and the unique challenges that survivors may face.

In order to best support survivors of gender-based violence, Christian counselors must be prepared to help clients develop coping strategies to manage the impact of the violence on their mental health. This may involve providing support and guidance around safety planning, connecting clients with community resources, and working collaboratively with other professionals, such as law enforcement and medical providers. Additionally, counseling sessions may need to be tailored to address the unique psychological needs of survivors, including feelings of guilt, shame, and self-blame.

It is also important to recognize that gender-based violence can have a long-term impact on a survivor's mental health and well-being. As such, Christian counselors should be prepared to offer ongoing support to clients as they navigate the aftermath of the violence. This may involve regular counseling sessions, referrals to support groups, and ongoing monitoring of the client's mental health.

Overall, it is crucial for Christian counselors to be well-informed about the impact of gender based violence on mental health and to be prepared to provide compassionate and effective support to survivors. By working collaboratively with other professionals and providing a safe and supportive environment for clients, Christian counselors can play a critical role in helping survivors of gender-based violence heal and move forward with their lives.

Clients who are struggling with gender identity concerns may experience significant distress and may benefit from support and guidance from a Christian counselor. This may include providing education and support around gender identity and expression, exploring the impact of societal expectations and norms, and helping clients navigate the process of coming out to friends and family.

In addition, Christian counselors can help clients identify and develop coping strategies to manage difficult emotions and situations related to their gender identity. This may involve exploring and processing past experiences, identifying personal strengths and resources, and building resilience.

Furthermore, Christian counselors can work collaboratively with other professionals, such as medical providers and therapists who specialize in gender identity concerns, to provide comprehensive care to clients. This may include coordinating care plans, providing referrals to appropriate resources and services, and ensuring that clients receive the support they need to thrive.

Sexism, or discrimination based on gender, is a pervasive issue that can affect people of all genders. It can manifest in various forms, from subtle microaggressions to overt acts of violence, and can have a profound impact on mental health and well-being. Christian counselors have an important role to play in addressing the impact of sexism on their clients' mental health.

To do this effectively, counselors must be prepared to engage in open and honest conversations with their clients about their experiences of sexism. This can involve creating a safe and non-judgmental environment where clients feel comfortable sharing their stories. Counselors can then work collaboratively with clients to help them develop coping strategies to manage the impact of these experiences on their mental health.

One strategy counselors can use is to explore the impact of societal expectations and norms on their clients' experiences of sexism. By examining how traditional gender roles and stereotypes influence our perceptions and interactions with others, clients can gain a deeper understanding of how sexism operates in their lives. Counselors can also help clients challenge negative self-talk and internalized sexism by providing them with tools and techniques to counter these harmful thought patterns.

In addition, counselors can provide education and support around gender equality and feminism. This can involve discussing the history of the feminist movement, exploring the ways in which gender inequality manifests in different contexts, and highlighting the importance of gender diversity and inclusivity.

Overall, by taking a holistic and client-centered approach, Christian counselors can help their clients navigate the complex and often challenging terrain of sexism and its impact on mental health and well-being.

Some examples of gender-related concerns that Christian counselors may encounter include:

- A transgender client who is struggling with discrimination and harassment in the workplace
- A woman who has experienced sexual assault and is struggling with symptoms of PTSD
- A male client who is struggling with body image concerns and has developed an eating disorder
- A non-binary client who is feeling isolated and unsupported by their family and community
- A client who is struggling with internalized sexism and negative self-talk related to their gender

In conclusion, gender is an important consideration in Christian counseling. By understanding and addressing the ways in which gender identity, gender expression, sexism, and gender-based violence can impact mental health and well-being, Christian counselors can provide more effective and compassionate care to clients.

Chapter 15: Conclusion and Future Directions

15.1 Summary of the Manual

This manual has provided a comprehensive overview of the key considerations that Christian counselors need to keep in mind while working with clients from diverse backgrounds. While the importance of cultural competency, socioeconomic status, and gender in the counseling process has been explored in depth, there are other factors that are equally relevant and must be considered.

One such factor is age. It is essential for counselors to recognize that clients from different age groups have unique needs, preferences, and expectations, and that these factors can significantly impact the counseling process. Moreover, counselors must be aware of the various life transitions that individuals go through as they move from one stage of life to another, and the impact that these transitions can have on their mental health and well-being.

Another important factor that has not been discussed in detail so far is the role of family and community in the counseling process. While a client-centered approach is essential, it is equally important to recognize the impact that family dynamics, cultural norms, and community expectations can have on a client's mental health and well-being. Counselors must be willing to engage with these external factors and work collaboratively with clients and their support systems to promote healing and growth.

Furthermore, the importance of addressing issues related to social justice and advocacy cannot be overstated. Christian counselors have a unique opportunity to leverage their position to promote social change and advocate for marginalized communities. By recognizing the systemic barriers that exist in our society and working to dismantle them, counselors can play a crucial role in promoting healing and transformation in their communities.

Throughout this manual, we have emphasized the need for a holistic and client-centered approach to counseling. By acknowledging and respecting the unique experiences and perspectives of each individual client, counselors can create a safe and supportive environment that encourages growth, healing, and transformation. By incorporating the key considerations discussed in this manual, counselors can provide effective and sensitive counseling to clients from diverse backgrounds, and promote positive change in their communities.

15.2 Future Directions for Christian Counseling

Looking ahead, there are several exciting directions that Christian counseling can explore in order to continue its growth and evolution. One of the most important areas of focus is the incorporation of technology into the counseling process. With the rise of teletherapy and other digital tools, Christian counselors have the opportunity to connect with clients in new and innovative ways. By embracing technology, counselors can provide more accessible and convenient care to individuals who may not have been able to access counseling services in the past, and can explore new ways to support their clients' mental health.

In addition to technology, Christian counseling can explore the development of new approaches to counseling that are more inclusive and sensitive towards the diverse backgrounds of clients. Counselors may consider incorporating practices that cater specifically to the experiences of people from underrepresented groups such as people of color, the LGBTQ+ community, and those with disabilities. By doing so, counselors can develop strategies that are more effective in addressing the unique challenges that clients from diverse backgrounds may face. For example, Christian counselors can explore the use of culturally sensitive interventions that incorporate the client's cultural beliefs and values into the counseling process.

Another important area of growth for Christian counseling is the continued development of evidence-based practices. While Christian counseling has traditionally relied on faith-based approaches to treatment, a growing body of research has shown that evidence-based practices can be effective in improving mental health outcomes. By engaging in rigorous research and evaluation, Christian counselors can ensure that they are providing the most effective and evidence-based care possible to their clients. Counselors can also collaborate with other professionals in the field to share their findings and to further advance research in the area of Christian counseling. By doing so, they can contribute to the development of a more robust and evidence-based approach to Christian counseling.

In conclusion, Christian counseling is a field that continues to evolve and grow. By exploring new directions and approaches, Christian counselors can provide the most effective, compassionate, and client-centered care possible, while also contributing to the advancement of the field as a whole. The development of evidence-based practices, collaboration with other professionals, and the incorporation of technology are all exciting directions that Christian counseling can continue to pursue in order to improve mental health outcomes for individuals and communities.